THE
IMPRESSIONISTS

BY

FRANÇOIS MATHEY

Translated by Jean Steinberg

FREDERICK A. PRAEGER, *Publisher*

NEW YORK

BOOKS THAT MATTER
Published in the United States of America in 1961
by Frederick A. Praeger, Inc., Publisher
64 University Place, New York 3, N. Y.
All rights reserved
Library of Congress catalog card number 61-5759

THE IMPRESSIONISTS
is published in two editions:

A Praeger Paperback (PPS-50)
A clothbound edition

PRINTED IN FRANCE

CONTENTS

COROT. THE GUST OF WIND. G. RENAND COLLECTION, PARIS.

INTRODUCTION

A new work on Impressionism cannot claim to throw new light on a subject which has been repeatedly and thoroughly discussed and written about.   Attitudes toward and ideas about art, like every-thing else, undergo changes, modifications, and shifts of emphasis. Today, we look upon the Impressionists not only as revolutionaries who defied the academic traditions of their age, not only as the successors of Delacroix, Courbet, and Corot, but also as the prophets and precursors of modern painting. Impressionism heralded a new attitude toward art. The Impressionist, in overthrowing the old, gave birth to a new tradition.

Around 1860, a group of young artists of diverse backgrounds and origins who were living and studying in Paris joined together informally to find new forms and new approaches in painting. They had met each other in the studio of Gleyre, at the Académie Suisse, at the École des Beaux-Arts. These artists who, years later, were to be derisively dubbed Impressionists by their opponents, were far less concerned with a particular style of painting than with a communal attitude toward certain fundamental problems, such as light and color. They left their studios and went to the forest of Fontainebleau, to the banks of the Oise, to Normandy in order

HARPIGNIES. FISHERMEN IN A LANDSCAPE.
CABINET DES DESSINS, LOUVRE, PARIS.

THE SALON OF 1857 IN THE PALAIS DE L'INDUSTRIE, PARIS.

to paint in the open air. When a group that included Monet, Renoir, Pissarro, Sisley, Degas, Cézanne, and Berthe Morisot organized its first exhibit in 1874, in defiance of the official Salon, their contemporaries—accustomed as they were to the use of varnish, to patina and chiaroscuro—considered these new painters anarchistic lunatics, "intoxicated" revolutionaries. They were indeed intoxicated, but with their rediscovery of light as the primal source of painting. By their affirmation of the primacy of light, they revitalized the concept of the pictorial element inherent

3

in color. This affirmation brought in its wake new techniques, a new language—simpler, more direct, more immediate, more meaningful.

The passage of time and the attempts of art historians to give logic and coherence to a system that, by its very nature, defies analysis have given rise to the false conception of Impressionism as an autonomous entity. What the Impressionists had in common was their vocabulary of form and their love of independence. Impressionism was primarily the symbol of a liberation, of an emancipation from the rigidities of the Salon. As far as style and technique are concerned, any attempt to find a unifying element between Monet and Cézanne, between Renoir and Degas, or between Manet and Pissarro would be doomed to failure. As Lionello Venturi said: "Renoir expresses all the happiness, the vitality, and the humor of his subject; Monet the essence of things; Degas the mastery, calculated in every detail; Cézanne the grandeur, the subtlety, and the science; Pissarro the rustic faith and the epic breadth; Sisley the delicacy and repose." But in their friendship

DIAZ. THE OAKS. CABINET DES DESSINS, LOUVRE, PARIS.

4

BONINGTON. PARTERRE D'EAU, VERSAILLES. 1826. LOUVRE, PARIS.

A sky, broadly painted like a Tiepolo, sheds a light that seems to presage a storm. It is an oil painting executed with the freedom and dash of a water color. Bonington's facility in the latter medium is, in fact, apparent in his use of oils: his preference for bright and fluid tones, for reflections and transparency. Both concept and execution bear almost no trace of Romanticism; the whole atmosphere is new, not only reminiscent of both Turner and Delacroix, but also foreshadowing Manet. Light is the dominant feature, and it is this quality which gives the work its astonishing freshness.

JULES GARNIER. JETSAM. EXHIBITED IN THE SALON OF 1873.

for each other and in their struggle against all formalism and academic rules, they were as one.

TRADITIONS AND INNOVATIONS. There was a time when the arts—sponsored and supported by a small, select, refined group—reflected aristocratic tastes and interests. But the spread of industrialism and mercantilism created a new bourgeoisie that was sufficiently strong to assume the once-traditional role of the nobility as sponsors of art. A society chiefly motivated by profit, power, and comfort had, of course, little use for artistic integrity and imaginative creativity. The bourgeoisie sought and found painters able to translate its values into pictures, thus giving rise to a school of art replete with banality and vapid themes, to a

6

saccharine romanticism which delighted in such subjects as *Entering the Convent, The Bathing Venus, Grenadiers on the Road from Magenta.* Landscapes other than those set amidst mythological or historical scenes were frowned upon; portraiture, skillfully executed and "beautiful", enjoyed popularity. A certain degree of originality was tolerated and accepted, but only if the artist was careful not to transcend the boundaries of conventionality. The Romanticists, drawing on medieval legends for their motifs, did try to evade the issue. But no artist can successfully escape the age in which he lives—at best, he can reject it.

By the middle of the nineteenth century, "respectable" paintings and artists were much in vogue in Paris salons. Elegant, airy portraits by Dubufe, dignified and pompous ones by Bonnat, distin-

COURBET. GIRLS ON THE BANKS OF THE SEINE. PEN DRAWING.

COURBET. TWO GIRLS
ON THE BANKS OF THE SEINE. 1856.
MUSÉE DES BEAUX-ARTS, PARIS.

Courbet, whom Zola called the "creator of flesh," spread his colors as if he were sculpting a thigh or a breast. Here were echoes of Rubens; not until Renoir would there be another artist with the same feeling for women, the same sensuality. Courbet's great innovation was the discovery and introduction of open-air painting as a genre and method different from traditional landscape painting. A peasant and a hunter, he was bound to feel confined by the walls of his studio, and he had too much love and respect for nature to recreate it from memory. He took his easel to the banks of the Loue and the Seine and to the woods at Ornans. He painted all his landscapes in this way, but he added the figures later in the studio; indeed they often seem to be an adjunct to ehe composition as a whole. Manet, tollowing Courbet's example, painttd the background of the Déjeuner sur l'Herbe *at Gennevilliers, but only made sketches for the nude figure. He did not paint her on the spot; hence this painting produced the same abrupt effect as Courbet's.*

8

THÉODORE ROUSSEAU. LANDSCAPE. CABINET DES DESSINS, LOUVRE, PARIS.

guished, worldly likenesses by Carolus-Duran and Flameng were greatly admired. The patriotic fervor of the times found expression in the quasi-epic military canvases of Yvon, Pils, Detaille, and especially Meissonier, of whose paintings Degas said, "Everything was heavy except the armor."

It has ever been the classic pastime of the academies to create the illusion of preserving a cultural heritage—frequently one not their own—and the official Salon followed this tradition, upholding the

COROT. THE LITTLE SHEPHERD. C. 1855.
CABINET DES DESSINS, LOUVRE, PARIS.

conventional ideals of the glory of France. The public usually
wants the familiar; it wants the soothing, satisfying reassurance of
having its taste confirmed and certified by a higher authority. It

Not until after the Paris Salon of 1824 was Constable, hitherto considered a minor master, recognized in England as a great painter. The traditional, carefully composed, historical, literary landscape became, after him, nothing more than an obsolete convention, a museum piece ; his new, modern, and honest vision had a profound effect on all painters, in particular on the French landscape painters of the 1830's. In Constable's mature work there are no echoes of Ruysdael, Claude Lorrain, or Gainsborough ; there is only that genuine feeling and love which he experienced when, for the first time, he set up his easel in front of nature. He, who so vehemently objected to having old, smoky, and dirty canvases represent the works of God, already saw with the eyes of an Impressionist. He was a precursor of Boudin and Claude Monet, and it is hardly surprising

CONSTABLE. BRIGHTON BEACH. 1824. VICTORIA AND ALBERT MUSEUM, LONDON.

DELACROIX. VIEW OF THE SEA, DIEPPE. 1854. PRIVATE COLLECTION, PARIS.

that he exerted great influence on Delacroix, who, after seeing Constable's works in 1824, repainted the landscape in his Massacres of Scio. *Admittedly Delacroix, though almost thirty years younger, seems more romantic than Constable, but both of them shared that same love of the open air and of light, both sought contrasts with an eye to the intensification of color. Fired by the desire "to achieve an even greater brilliance and luminosity," Delacroix augmented his still somber palette with pure tones which, refusing to use flat colors, he juxtaposed in infinite gradations. As other artists went further along the same road, Delacroix was hailed first by the Impressionists and later by the Neo-Impressionists, who considered him their earliest precursor.*

13

does not want to be surprised; it hates the unexpected; it fears being duped. At a time when bourgeois conformity was at its height, when Paul Baudry's copies of Boucher's cupids decorated the canopy of Empress Eugénie's bed, Manet's *Olympia,* gently reclining on her couch, startled and shocked middle-class sensibilities; she seemed to be the goddess of a new revolutionary cult.

The apparently uninterrupted artistic tradition of France is, of course, nothing more than a series of breaks with the past, of new discoveries and trail-blazing innovations. It is the constant affirmation of an individual creativity faithful to its art rather than to formalistic, obsolete rules. It is a tradition of freedom, and established society finds freedom disturbing. Tradition, properly understood, is by no means synonymous with repetition, but its self-appointed guardians invariably equate tradition with repetition. No wonder, then, that the Impressionists were accused of wishing to destroy the established order, the noble heritage of France.

The École des Beaux-Arts, the Academy of Fine Arts, M. de Nieuwekerke as the Imperial Director of Fine Arts, the biennial Salons—all these were the official arbiters of what was art, of what was worth exhibiting, of who was to be rewarded. The Academy selected the Beaux-Arts teachers and appointed the official jury of the Salons. Thus, it is not at all surprising that in 1857 the jury rejected *The Morning Star* by Chaplin, excellent artist though he was, because he had dared paint a nude not to be found in the pages of mythology—neither Diana nor Venus, but just a nude. And ten years later, at the Salon of 1867, the coveted prizes were still being awarded to such reliable traditionalists as Meissonier, Cabanel, and Gérôme.

The art world did, of course, know of the existence of the so-called Barbizon School of landscape painters. Though it was admitted that the Barbizon painters did evince some feeling for

DELACROIX. LANDSCAPE. CABINET DES DESSINS, LOUVRE, PARIS.

nature, their paintings were considered quite insignificant and
secondary: the subjects were, after all, simply trees, glades, and
wooded paths, devoid of nymphs or shepherds or people. And it
came as no surprise that their admirers included revolutionaries
and anti-traditionalists like Gautier, Baudelaire, and Claretie. The
Barbizon style was said to be vulgar and pretentious, bordering on
the doctrinaire, and when—as in the case of Millet—it toyed with
philosophical approaches, the works became ugly and fraudulent.
Contemporary critics charged that Millet did not understand the
beauty of rural life; that he failed to imbue his landscapes with
human feeling. How different was the work of decent, reliable
painters like Jules Breton, with his *Gleaners of Artois*—visual proof

TURNER. VENICE: THE PIAZZETTA FROM THE WATER. C. 1838-1840.
TATE GALLERY, LONDON.

As early as 1835, Turner, with his Norham Castle, Sunrise, *had
heralded the Impressionism of Claude Monet.   In this "vision" of
Venice—one can no longer call it a "view"—painted during his
third and last visit to that city, the painter, dazzled and intoxicated
by the light and the color, approaches the sublime.   The subject
fades away, dissolves in the vibrations of the colors.   All that
remains is a fairy-like, cosmic impression of nature.   Turner followed no theories, only his own artistic intuition.   As far back as 1816,
William Hazlitt had described Turner's works as "paintings
representing the elements of air, earth, and water."   His late works
were criticized because they represented objects " by a scale of yellow,
scarlet, orange, and sky blue which exists only in his imagination and*

is accepted solely because of the tolerance of his admirers." A pre-cursor of lyrical abstraction, Turner's art foreshadowed that of a Victor Pasmore or a Philip Guston. Monet, on the other hand, followed a theoretical program, but his creative instinct was stronger than his theory. Like Turner, he was the primitive of a new abstract world, and again like Turner, he allowed himself to be carried away and achieved the same pure lyricism. Monet, who had discovered the magic of the great English landscape painter in 1870, returned to London several times between 1899 and 1905 and visited Venice in 1908-1909. Though more than half a century separated them, the spectacle of the sun-drenched lagoon filled both artists with the same wonder. What mattered, over and above the subject chosen, was the vibration of color and space, the lightness of the atmosphere and the sparkle of the water.

MONET. THE PALACE OF THE DOGES SEEN FROM SAN GIORGIO. 1908.
DURAND-RUEL COLLECTION, PARIS.

17

that painting can be both pleasant and moral. Thus, narrow-mindedness and stupidity degraded painting to the level of reproductions, of portraits for conference rooms and ballroom ceilings, of painted screens, fans, and saucers, of pictures fit for prefectures and bachelor flats. For an artist to proclaim the sacredness of painting, to maintain that color was all—important and the subject merely a pretext, to dare disregard the École des Beaux-Arts and its teachers and work in the open air like a fisherman instead of studying the languid pose of a model in a studio, to prefer painting nudes under trees instead of draping them in red velvet—all this was an affront to morality, an outrageous insult to the memory of the Greeks and Romans, to stability and tradition, to Raphael.

DAUBIGNY. VILLAGE ON THE BANKS OF A CANAL. CABINET DES DESSINS, LOUVRE, PARIS.

MILLET. SCREEN OF TREES. CABINET DES DESSINS, LOUVRE, PARIS.

This was the unforgivable sin committed by the Impressionists.
There is a tendency to label all French painting between 1870
and 1890 as Impressionist. This has some validity, since Impressionism was the only important contribution to art during that
period. But we tend to forget that Impressionism, even after its
reluctant acceptance, remained a fringe movement. A glance at
the art reviews of the period furnishes convincing proof of how
small a place was occupied by the Impressionists. And this is
true despite the fact that there were many more painters in the
movement than are remembered today. To be a member of the
avant-garde does not automatically bestow immortality upon an artist.
Who today remembers Béliard, Attendu, Brandon, Bureau, Colin,

*A beautiful, slender, naked girl on soft, white cushions.   She is not
yet twenty.   Her name is Olympia.   She knows life and cannot
even imagine a world free of privation, unpaid bills, alcohol, and
casual liaisons.   But she has lovers and this reassuring certainty
fulfills the needs of her body.   In the depths of the alcove, a large
Negress in a pink dress holds a magnificent bouquet of blue flowers.
A black cat arches itself—in other words, the conventional theme of
the eternal odalisque which has always, from Titian to Matisse,
exerted a fascination over painters ; such a banal theme, in fact, that
Manet had no reason whatsoever to foresee the furore this traditional
figure would provoke.   There were illustrious predecessors: Titian,
whose famous* Venus of Urbino *he had copied in 1853, and Goya,
whose* Maja *he must certainly have known.   Moreover, if the theme
was objectionable, it is difficult to see why the same indignation was
not aroused some years later at the Salon of 1868 by Jules Lefebvre's*

MANET. STUDY FOR "OLYMPIA." CABINET DES DESSINS, LOUVRE, PARIS.

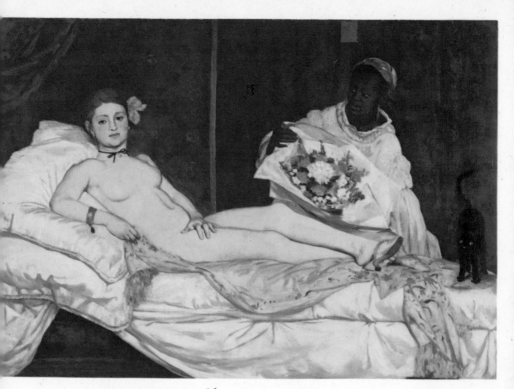

MANET. OLYMPIA. 1863. LOUVRE, PARIS.

Odalisque, *a large canvas in "museum style" which was a replica,
albeit a very academic one, of the* Olympia. *But the real issue was
the artist's concept, and because Manet's solution was unconventional it was reprehensible. It took daring to give such importance to
a single figure dominating a canvas of these dimensions. But that was
the point: a uniformly bright area on another light tone, set against a
dark, yet expressively executed, background. The technique of
merely suggesting volume by a line without exact modeling was
opposed to all existing principles ; but Manet had learned from the
Japanese that outline, be it sensitive or unobtrusive, brutal or volup-
tuous, defines volume and thus gives forms an immediate impact. It
was a lesson which he handed on to Gauguin, who made a copy of
Manet's* Olympia *in the Louvre.*

21

Cordey, Latouche, Legros, Lepic, De Molins, Ottin ? There were more than twenty of them who, after the Impressionist exhibition of 1874, considered themselves members of the movement, but who today are looked upon as artistic nonentities. Novel techniques are not to be confused with originality. The Impressionists had neither charter nor studio nor school; at best, they formed a sort of family. At times, the novelty of their approach may have led their contemporaries into putting technique above inspiration, and it is by no means inconceivable that the Impressionists themselves became prisoners of their skill. However, their one common aim was to reproduce optical effects in accordance with the discoveries of modern physics. This method, so bravely rational and experimental, was destined to open up a whole new world of personal, subjective, magical emotions—the world of art rediscovered.

MILLET. NOVEMBER. CHARCOAL DRAWING. LOUVRE, PARIS.

PRECURSORS OF IMPRESSIONISM

THE English painter Turner was the first to abandon the dominant Dutch school for a new approach in landscape painting. He created landscapes suffused with mist and light—the antithesis of the soot, dirt, and oppressive closeness of city life. In these landscapes he sought to rediscover the divine light, the source of life. Turner's inspired canvases are like the paeans of a blind man who has regained the gift of sight. The English landscape painters had a deeply emotional, dynamic, almost religious appreciation of nature. The works of Constable, Bonington, Copley Fielding, Harding, Roberts, and Wyld—exhibited at the Paris Salon of 1824 —were in truly striking contrast to the popular romantic canvases of Michallon, Bertin, and Remon. "Air! Space!" exclaimed Delacroix, carried away by these "diamonds that enchant the eye, unhampered by subject, free of imitation."

Constable knew that no two days or two hours were ever alike, that in the whole of Creation there was no such thing as two identical leaves. Discovered in France and admired there before he gained recognition in England, Constable was almost obsessed by the constantly changing face of nature; his storm pictures were to make a deep impression on the Barbizon painters Huet, Dupré, and Théodore Rousseau. Géricault, while visiting London in 1820, was struck by the luminosity in the water colors of Constable,

Daumier did not devote himself fully to the lyrical aspect of painting until he was in his sixties. His enthusiasm and generous temperament expressed themselves in a very broad, impulsive treatment full of contrasts and, above all, in his exceptionally vigorous draftsmanship. His intensely

DAUMIER. THE WASHERWOMAN. PRIVATE COLLECTION, PARIS.

CÉZANNE. A MODERN OLYMPIA. 1872-1873. LOUVRE, PARIS.

baroque art reflects his southern exuberance in the same way as did the
early works of Cézanne.   Thus, when Cézanne, paying homage to Manet,
reverted to the theme of Olympia, the result was reminiscent of Daumier.
    It was in connection with this canvas that M. de Montifaud wrote in
1874: "This apparition of a scrap of pink, naked flesh . . . this corner
of an artificial paradise made even the bravest men choke, and M. Cézanne
seemed to have become simply a sort of madman, his painting activated by
delirium tremens."   Obsessed by his "complexes," Cézanne sought to free
himself of them by carrying out a series of somber, tormented canvases,
enlivened with large white flourishes.

25

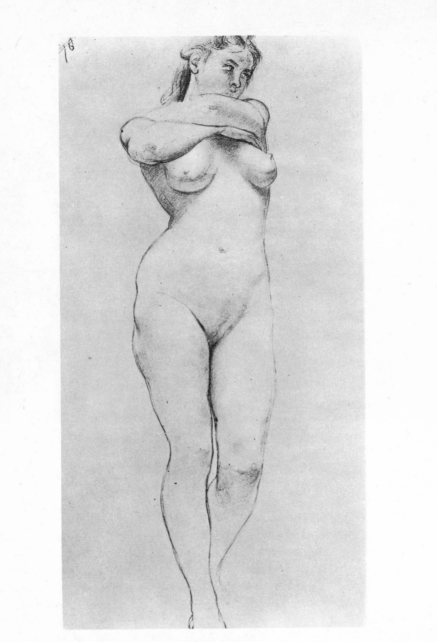

COROT. NUDE.
COLLECTION P. MCILHENNY, PHILADELPHIA.

COROT. OUTSKIRTS OF ROME. BIBLIOTHÈQUE NATIONALE, PARIS.

this self-designated "enemy of the old, dirty, smoky canvases."
Thus, Constable with his power of observation and Turner with his
visionary gift stood at the threshold of modern French landscape
painting.   Through them, Delacroix discovered that light dissolves
the object, a discovery that enabled him to become one of the first
painters to work with primary colors.   This technique, in turn,
helped pave the way for the experimentation of the Impressionists.

*Boudin was the Constantin Guys of the Normandy beaches. His
sketches quiver with sensibility ; the clouds move across the sky and
the sun plays among the crinolines. Everything is done with
lightness and elegance ; the tonal relationships are marvelously
exact and subtle. Boudin never pretended to be anything more than
a minor master following in the wake of the Dutch landscape painters.
His work is charming, lively, inimitable but slight. It is his
exquisite feeling for nature which carries him through. "The
romantics have had their day," he wrote, "henceforth one must seek
out the simple beauties of nature." It was in this spirit that he
instructed the young Monet, fifteen years his junior, when the latter
worked alongside him at Le Havre. Monet's own vision was both
more forceful and more modern, and perhaps he is indebted to Jongkind rather than to Boudin for his freedom of style, his broad, forth-
right treatment of his solidly composed pictures bathed in the limpid-
ity of the sea air and the lightness of the sky. That "daring manner
of seeing things and commanding the attention of the spectator,"*

BOUDIN. CRINOLINES ON THE BEACH. 1869. PRIVATE COLLECTION, PARIS.

MONET. HOTEL DES ROCHES-NOIRES, TROUVILLE. 1870.
J. LAROCHE COLLECTION, PARIS.

*as Paul Mantz said in 1865, is evident in the breeze that blows
the clouds accross the sky and flutters the flags, in the intensity of
the touch, and the emphasis of the light which breaks abruptly across
the shaded façade and animates the figures.*

Delacroix's technique, his new harmonies, his discovery of reflected light and of the role of complementary colors foreshadowed the work of Monet. "Gray is the enemy of all painting . . . . Everything in nature is a reflection . . . ," he wrote. Utilizing his studies of Constable, Vermeer, Titian, and Rubens as a basis, Delacroix formulated the major principles of color division, of

DAUMIER. THE TWO THIEVES AND THE DONKEY. CHARCOAL.

BAZILLE. LANDSCAPE. LOUVRE, PARIS.

contrasting and complementary colors. (Many years later, the
Neo-Impressionists were to systematize these principles: "Green
and violet: these colors must be applied separately, one after the

other; they cannot be mixed on the palette. . . . It is not advisable to merge colors on the canvas. Seen from a distance, they will merge by themselves.") Thus, he arrived at the belief that reality must subordinate itself to inspiration, provided the artist has an awareness of the emotional impact of color: "Give me the dirt of the streets, and with it I will paint the delicate flesh-tones of a woman." Delacroix proved that an artist can interpret nature unhampered by convention and traditional viewpoints. Cézanne, in later years, was to remember this.

Daumier—defier of convention, an outsider seeking to break through the barriers of tradition—was still another champion of the omnipotence of imagination. His refusal to compromise contributed to the emancipation of the artist. True, his contemporaries failed to recognize his importance; to them, he was just a caricaturist, and the preconception that only large canvases could constitute great art relegated caricature to the realm of minor artistic endeavor. But his friends—among them Corot and Rousseau—realized that he was no mere cartoonist. "This fellow has something of Michelangelo in him," said Balzac, and Baudelaire called him "one of the most important figures in modern art." There is no doubt that Daumier had found a new way of looking at reality. In his role of caricaturist, he was accustomed to interpreting his subjects freely; in his role of sculptor, he was accustomed to working with solid materials, imbuing them with a sense of rhythm and a power of suggestion which transcended mere imitation. No one was further removed from the concept of art for art's sake; no one had greater awareness of the needs of his time. With his absolutely modern viewpoint, Daumier captured the essential, eternally valid characteristic.

Daumier's relationship to the society he satirized was not unlike Corot's intimate relationship to nature. Both painters, in their

BAZILLE. PORTRAIT OF RENOIR. 1867. MUSÉE DES BEAUX-ARTS, ALGIERS.

own individual ways, were concerned with the rediscovery of the harmony between man and his world, the source of all truth. Corot's contemporaries ignored and misunderstood him. It was the Impressionnists who harked back to his work, perhaps not so much because of the impeccable perfection of his technique, but rather because of his beautifully thought-out composition, which creates the illusion of a miraculously spontaneous encounter with nature. Corot was extremely concerned with this seemingly simple effect—an exterior behind which, modestly concealed, lies a highly intellectual conception. He seemed to pretend simply to put on canvas an image that he had carried within himself, to paint, effortlessly, something which he himself did not take quite seriously. His is the conflict of the modest man afraid of adventure. In his diary, Delacroix has noted down some of the advice given him by Corot: "He has told me to move ahead and surrender myself to whatever may lie ahead; that is what he does as a rule.... He refuses to admit that beauty can be created through endless

JONGKIND. SANNOIS. 1852. CABINET DES DESSINS, LOUVRE, PARIS.

DAUMIER. CLOWN. 1868. METROPOLITAN MUSEUM OF ART, NEW YORK.

effort." Delacroix did not care to heed this advice, but the Impressionists believed in the value of "whatever may lie ahead," and, like Corot, they mistrusted everything that did not appear effortless, as if created amid the illusion of happiness.

After a stay in Holland in *1871*, Monet settled in a house at Argenteuil which he loved because of its big garden where the children frolicked along the paths and among the bushes. Still dominated by memories of Manet, this picture is one of the last of the transitional period which preceded his orthodox Impressionism. Although painted in the open air, it gives the impression of having been done in the studio. The air is motionless, the light itself is merely a lighting effect, and Monet still uses it in a conventional manner. Later, when painting a landscape, he became much freer. He was undoubtedly ill at ease with portraits, as if the human figure were an accident interposing itself between the artist and nature.

MONET. JEAN MONET ON HIS WOODEN HORSE. 1872.
NATHAN CUMMINGS COLLECTION, CHICAGO.

*Renoir was the first to introduce the theme of the clown into painting ;
it was taken up again, with different emphasis, by Seurat, and later
by Toulouse-Lautrec.*

2

THE IMPRESSIONISTS MEET

IMPRESSIONISM was fired by the spirit of youthful creativity. Never before in the history of art had a group of young, inspired painters befriended each other, worked together so fruitfully, and eventually achieved immortality as a group. Though profoundly different in character, Manet and Degas were united in deep friendship, as were Monet, Bazille, Pissarro, Sisley, and Renoir. It almost seems that here was one of those rare moments in history when everything conspires to assure the triumph of an idea. The friendship that bound these men was far more than the casual acquaintance made in studios and cafés; it had the force of a commitment, the durability to survive quarrels as well as marriages, failure as well as success. In the search for a definition of Impressionism, perhaps this bond is of even greater importance than the artistic and aesthetic delights found in the group's work. And perhaps Impressionism represents nothing more, nothing else than the history of these friendships, with painting as its common denominator.

THE YOUNG CLAUDE MONET AND HIS CIRCLE. In 1859, the young Claude Monet came to Paris—a bit lost, but full of enthusiasm. Soon he was to become *the* master. He had met the already established marine painter Boudin in Le Havre, and the friendliness and honesty of the older painter had soon won

PISSARRO. RUE SAINT-VINCENT IN MONTMARTRE. 1860. PRIVATE COLLECTION, NEW YORK.

him over. He heeded Boudin's advice: "Study, learn to see and paint, draw, do landscapes. The ocean and the sky, animals, people, and trees—just as nature created them—are so beautiful in their own setting of light and air, just as they are. . . . All that is painted directly, at a given moment, has a force, power, and vitality which can never be duplicated in a studio." Boudin liked to take Monet along when he painted in the open air, but theirs never became a teacher-pupil relationship; Boudin was too modest for that, and Monet too independent. However, it took no great effort to convince Monet that he was born to be a painter. "It suddenly seemed," he said, "as if a veil were torn off. I under-

In his account of the Salon of 1870, Théodore Duret wrote: "In one aspect of his work, Pissarro is a realist. He would never rearrange nature to suit his composition. For him, a landscape on canvas must be an exact reproduction of a natural scene." Pissarro loved the countryside, the simple, rustic life evoked by stone houses and orchards. He loved walking along the by-roads which led to adventure. For him there were no problems of composition, but merely a concern to translate very prosaically that faith which the artist feels in a setting of peaceful nature bathed in a gentle, restrained light. Sisley and Monet were the painters of water, Pissarro the painter of the land.

PISSARRO. THE ROAD. 1870. LOUVRE, PARIS.

JONGKIND. DEMOLITION, RUE DES FRANCS-BOURGEOIS. 1868. GEMEENTEMUSEUM, THE HAGUE.

Impressionism is one of the most striking and wonderful creations of French art, but it needed the contributions of several foreign artists to enable it to blossom forth: Jongkind was Dutch, Sisley English, Pissarro came from the Antilles, and Cézanne himself was of Italian descent. The last of the minor Dutch masters, Jongkind broke away from genre painting. His subject was nature just as he found it, chill and wan, with its dockers, its coal yards, and its smoking factories. His influence on the young Impressionists was considerable, equal to that of Boudin and Courbet; it was in his footsteps that they discovered Montmartre and the gray-and-pink charm of the old streets of Paris.

41

stood what painting could be. . . . My future—becoming a painter—opened up for me."

So it was that, instead of going into his father's grocery business, Monet had come to Paris. Not for a moment did he consider enrolling in the École des Beaux-Arts. He haunted the studios of Armand Gautier, Lhuillier, Troyon; he learned to judge, to compare, to criticize. Ultimately, he did enroll in a school—the Académie Suisse—and not having any sponsor of note, he attached himself to Pissarro. The following year became one of glorious discovery for the young painter fresh from the provinces. His new, fascinating life was interrupted by the outbreak of the Franco-Prussian War and his consequent conscription for Army service. But providence, in the guise of typhoid fever, intervened, and he was able to return to Paris in November, 1862, full of self-confidence and the determination to succeed. In order to placate his father, who simply refused to believe in serious study without the supervision of an experienced teacher, he agreed to become a pupil of Gleyre, to whom his cousin Toulemouche had sent him. "You must go to Gleyre. He is the master of all of us. He'll teach you to paint a picture." Gleyre was a decent enough man, but his instruction could not possibly benefit any disciple of Boudin. Monet was criticized by Gleyre for reproducing his models too realistically: "Your model is a heavy-set man, and so you paint a heavy-set man. He has enormous feet, and you paint them just as they are. That, my friend, is ugly. You simply have to keep antiquity in mind when you paint. Nature is all right as an element of study, but aside from that it holds no interest. Style is the thing that matters, nothing but style !" In his own way, Monet, of course, was also concerned with style. How about Millet, Corot, Delacroix, Courbet, he asked himself; didn't they have style ? Did one always have to copy, to plagiarize ? Monet knew that he was not cut out to be a follower of styles. Jules

PISSARRO. STUDY OF TREES. CABINET DES DESSINS, LOUVRE, PARIS.

Breton, F.-L. Français, Bastien-Lepage, and Benjamin Constant were of no interest to him; he had no intention of becoming just another painter who, incapable of original work, made his living by imitating his teachers. He saw no hope for his own artistic development in working along established lines; he was convinced of the necessity of finding a fresh approach. The death of Delacroix in 1863 spelled the end of one generation of painters. Monet, just turned twenty-three, felt that the time had come to take up the cudgels on behalf of the new, and a small group of friends from Gleyre's studio were ready to lend him their support. They were Bazille, Renoir, and Sisley—and they, too, were unappreciated and impatient.

43

La Grenouillère, on the banks of the Seine, was almost a branch of the Café Guerbois; here, the painters and their women friends used to meet on Sundays. Monet, who lived nearby, came there often to meet Renoir. Water, whose reflections seem to dissolve reality, never ceased to exercise a singular attraction over Monet throughout the whole of his long career. John Rewald, in his The History of Impressionism, *notes: "Just as snow scenes had permitted the artists to investigate the problems of shadows, the study of water offered an excellent opportunity to observe reverberations and reflections. Thus they could further develop their knowledge of the fact that so-called local color was actually a pure convention and that every object presents to the eye a scheme of color derived from its*

MONET. THE LAKE AT ARGENTEUIL. C. 1874.
SCHOOL OF DESIGN, PROVIDENCE, RHODE ISLAND.

MONET. LA GRENOUILLÈRE. 1869. METROPOLITAN MUSEUM OF ART, NEW YORK.

proper color, from its surroundings and from atmospheric conditions. Moreover, the study of water gave pretext for the representation of formless masses livened only by the richness of nuances, of large surfaces whose texture invited vivid brushstrokes." The need to render the constantly changing vibrations of light and water implied, in effect, a technique of its own, one of swift brushstrokes, of vivid, sparkling dots and lines. During the five years that separated these two works, Monet had gained assurance and matured. One might possibly confuse some of the works of Monet and Renoir painted at La Grenouillère at that period, even though Monet's were more powerful and bolder in execution ; by 1874, such a mistake was no longer possible. The problem of technique had, for Monet, been solved and left behind. Nothing remained but an intimate communion between the artist and nature.

Frédéric Bazille was the son of a well-to-do Montpellier family.
Bored with his medical studies, his real interest lay in painting, to
which the collector Bruyas, a friend of his parents and of Courbet,
had introduced him. Monet's fiery temperament attracted this
young man from the south of France. Sisley, whose British
elegance and sense of propriety were outraged by the vulgar
atmosphere of the studios, was impressed with Monet's sincerity,
his strength of character, and his artistic vision. Renoir, less
favored by fortune than were his friends, waged a hard struggle—
decorating endless series of plates, shades, fans, and madonnas for
his living—and truly earned his right to become a painter. He had
a burning desire to win recognition and approval, but as far as

SISLEY. THE BANKS OF THE LOING. ETCHING.

Gleyre was concerned, his innate sense of color was nothing but an irritating "vice." When Gleyre disdainfully asked Renoir whether he painted for his own amusement, Renoir replied that were it not for that, he wouldn't paint; he then packed his easel and left. The break had been made.

The four friends decided to look elsewhere for that truth which Boudin had promised Monet, which Bazille had sensed in Courbet, which Renoir bore within himself like a terrible disease. Their first steps in that search for truth brought them to the old masters. "The Louvre! The Louvre! There is only the Louvre! You

The subtitles which Whistler gave his pictures—Harmony in
Gray and Green, Arrangement in Gray and Black, Nocturne
Blue and Gold, Symphony in White—*reveal his preoccupation
with lyrical and literary aspects rather than with pictorial qualities.*

WHISTLER. OLD BATTERSEA BRIDGE: NOCTURNE — BLUE AND GOLD.
C. 1865. TATE GALLERY, LONDON.

MONET. WESTMINSTER. 1871. LORD ASTOR COLLECTION, LONDON.

In the absence of stern discipline this is a dangerous road for an artist to follow. Carried away by the ease with which he worked, Whistler liked to create effects ; thus, ultimately, his work became largely decorative. Such a painter frequently succeeds in clarifying for the public the creative genius of the artist he copies. This interpretation constitutes Whistler's major contribution to Impressionism. But between Whistler's technical refinement, reminiscent of Japanese art, and Monet's delicacy lies the difference between an acquired skill and an artistically understood one. While in London in 1870, Monet painted this view of the Thames: an ageless work, sensitive, bathed in a light which dissolves all form. It comes as no surprise to find an echo of this method in a painter like Albert Marquet.

49

CLAUDE MONET. SEASCAPE. PEN DRAWING.

can never copy too much," Fantin-Latour told Renoir. Renoir turned to the eighteenth-century painters, those masterly proponents of feminine beauty; Bazille devoted himself to Rubens and Tintoretto. But Monet went out into the country. To him, the treasures of nature seemed far more precious than those enclosed within museum walls. He took his friends to Chailly on the edge of the Fontainebleau forest, near Barbizon. This flight from the city led to the first encounter of these young painters with the *plein air* motif; here, under the open sky, they found themselves being carried away by a sense of newly discovered freedom, they became intoxicated with what Théodore Rousseau had called the "virginal contact with nature." During this period, they came to know Corot, Daubigny, Millet, and Diaz. And when Diaz one day told Renoir, "This is not a bad drawing, but why the devil do you paint everything so black ?" he helped to seal Renoir's artistic fate. Renoir needed no further encouragement to discard all he had been taught in the studios, to lighten his palette, thus dismaying the more timid Sisley. "You are mad, really mad, to paint like this," Sisley told him. But Monet reassured him: "We are on the right way. We must not lose heart. We no longer have the right to stop."

ANOTHER GROUP: PISSARRO, GUILLAUMIN, AND CÉZANNE. Meanwhile, at the Académie Suisse, another circle had formed around Pissarro, Guillaumin, and Cézanne. Paul Cézanne, a not very enthusiastic law student at Aix-en-Provence, had finally managed to obtain his father's permission to visit his old school friend Émile Zola in Paris and study painting there. His first contact with Paris was to prove an unhappy experience. This shy yet passionate twenty-two-year-old, independent and obsessed by an inner vision, had great difficulty in adjusting to life in Paris. His painting, with its excessive impasto, seemed like a testimony to the frustration of the artist unable to capture the image of his tortured imagination on canvas. Even his well-wishers were alienated by his work. Deeply disappointed that the ties between him and Zola had somehow loosened—and also disappointed in himself—he returned to Aix, and in the solitude of his parent's country house he tried to discover the causes for his failure. With humility and honesty, he tried to face up to his shortcomings: "The line eludes me. . . . I have little emotion, and I am unable to express myself; I am like a man with a gold coin who doesn't know how to use it." He was aware of his need for rigid discipline, and in its pursuit he copied fashion illustrations from magazines as carefully as he did Delacroix, Manet, or El Greco. He wanted to be both skillful and efficient, but his genius was stronger than his good intentions. His originality and his sensitivity

JONGKIND. SUNSET ON THE MEUSE. C. 1866. GINETTE SIGNAC COLLECTION, PARIS.

In Jongkind's work there is the age-old memory of the Dutch seafarers who, along with their spices, brought back the Japanese prints and kakemonos which inspired the Delft potters at the end of the seventeenth century. His water colors, painted with rapid and subtle brushstrokes, have the same moving sincerity as those of a Hiroshigé, who, with a single stroke, manages to suggest a whole immense universe. Here there is no hesitation, no uncertainty, but a keen and swift vision which catches the essential characteristic with vigorous conciseness. Monet, also, was interested in the Japanese, but he went beyond the lesson that they had to teach until his memories of it almost became subconscious. The fleecy clouds, the gently rippling water, and the triangular sail suspended between sky and water impose their own slow rhythm on the composition. "This picture, ill-defined and crude, seems to us an affirmation of ignorance and a denial of beauty as well as truth. We are badgered enough with bogus eccentricity, and it is only too easy to catch people's attention by doing something worse than anyone has dared do it before." This was the verdict of Charivari on the 1874 exhibition. In Le Figaro the tone was much the same. Today, such reactions are hard to understand. However, the public then was no more stupid than our own; it was only that they were not yet able to see: ability to see—in the Impressionist sense—presupposes a knowledge of the intimate physical nature of things, and particularly of light, which is far more than a subtle interplay of delicate values. Intuitively, the painters had reached the same conclusions as did the scientists in their deductive reasoning. But the public, as if stricken with blindness, needed a long time to get used to it.

MONET. SAILBOAT AT ARGENTEUIL. C. 1874.
F. W. BRAVINGTON COLLECTION, HENLEY-ON-THAMES.

CÉZANNE. GATE TO A FARM AT AUVERS-SUR-OISE. C. 1873.
ETCHING. BIBLIOTHÈQUE NATIONALE, PARIS.

could find no outlet in techniques of the past. The Impressionists were to teach him the use of color, allowing him to benefit from their discoveries of a new optical truth. Ultimately, when Pissarro and Cézanne went to Pontoise and, following in the footsteps of Daubigny, to Auvers, Pissarro aroused Cézanne's interest in open-air painting.

3

SALON DES REFUSÉS,
A TURNING POINT FOR IMPRESSIONISM

As the time for the Salon of 1863 drew near, the government decided to reassert its power in matters of art. For the artist, the Salon was a matter of life or death; no artist could hope to achieve fame and fortune without exhibition of his work in the Salon. The jury was determined to prevent the sort of laxness which, in 1861, had been responsible for the acceptance of Manet's *Spanish Guitar Player*. The final decision on whose work was to be exhibited rested with M. Signal, professor at the École des Beaux-Arts, who exercised his powers so rigorously that more than 4,000 paintings were rejected. Rejections on such a wholesale scale were absolutely without precedent, and the Emperor himself decided to intervene. Because of his initiative, another exhibit, the *Salon des Refusés,* was to be opened at the same time as the official Salon. Of course, any artist willing to show his work together with others which had repeatedly and justifiably been rejected by the Institute ran the risk of public ridicule. However, the faint-hearted, fearful of offending the jury by exhibiting their rejected paintings, withdrew. Thus the field was left to the followers of Courbet: Whistler, Manet (with his *Déjeuner sur l'Herbe, Young Man in Costume of a Majo,* and *Mlle. V. in Costume of an Espada*), Jongkind, Pissarro, Bracquemond, Fantin-Latour, Gautier, Legros, Guillaumin, and Cézanne. The *Salon des Refusés* attracted a great deal of attention

The theme of snow had often been exploited by the Dutch and Flemish landscapists, but nearly always for its decorative or picturesque effect or for local color rather than for its pure pictorial value. It was not until Courbet that this motif made its appearance in France, and when the

SISLEY. SNOW AT LOUVECIENNES. 1878. LOUVRE, PARIS.

MONET. THE MAGPIE. 1869. PRIVATE COLLECTION, PARIS.

*master of Ornans took to it, it seemed absolutely new.   It was a new kind
of snow that the Impressionists painted—Monet's being light and airy, and
Sisley's intimate and almost chaste.   Snow offers a superb pretext for
bold technical innovations: to show that white is not white, that it has less
luminous intensity than any pure color, just as shadow is not absolutely dark
but colored.   It also made it easier to capture a fleeting impression or a
lingering reflection.   In any case, these experiments required some virtuosity
of execution.   This explains why minor Impressionists like Lebourg,
Lépine, and Guillaumin, wishing to prove their skill in the use of rose-
whites, blue-whites and violet-whites, did so many snow scenes.   On the
other hand, it is worth noting that when Cézanne, Van Gogh, and Gauguin
rejected Impressionism they also rejected the snow motif.*

DEGAS. PORTRAIT OF DURANTY. 1879. METROPOLITAN MUSEUM OF ART, NEW YORK.

—and laughter. "A man needs the strength of two to remain upright amidst this onslaught of thousands of fools who scoff at and debase everything," wrote Auriac in his review of the exhibit. Manet emerged triumphant, and also a few art critics found the occasion to voice their attitude toward these new artists. "Manet's talent has an astonishing determination; it has a cutting, sobering, and energetic quality which helps to explain his reserved, exultant, and impressionable nature," wrote one critic. This was the beginning, and it gave the group of young painters an unparalleled opportunity to take stock of their strength, particularly since their approach was appreciated by painters who worked in an academic-classical vein. The positive responses, though representing only a segment of the public and of the critics, encouraged these young revolutionaries and helped them to stand firm.

GROWTH AND DEVELOPMENT. Bazille, Renoir, Monet, and Sisley—all refugees from Gleyre's studio—had become convinced of the futility of continuing with formal instruction. In 1864, Monet decided to settle in Honfleur, where Jongkind and Boudin were living at the time. There they were joined by Bazille, and the frequent, lively discussions of this group invariably centered around the problem of composition. Monet, unwilling to compromise, defended the realistic representation of the subject; Boudin, more conciliatory, was willing to grant that omission of details and rearrangement of lines were permissible; and Jongkind, always impulsive, championed complete freedom of composition, maintaining that the artist was free not only to omit but, if necessary, to add, according to the dictates of his inspiration. "I love this Jongkind," Castagnary had said in 1863. "He is an artist to his very fingertips, possessed of true and rare sensitivity. His work is all *impression*." Just as Constable and Boudin had done before him, Jongkind discovered how the so-called "local color" changes with the seasons. He had become aware of this after painting two identical pictures of the apse of Notre-Dame at different times—one in the cold, nacrous light of a winter morning, the other in the fiery glow of a sunset. It suddenly came to him that for the artist appearance, not reality, was the determining factor, that the subject was of no importance at all, and that the only thing that did matter was the atmospheric condition at a given moment. He shared this revelation with Monet, who, in turn, experimented by making two paintings of a road in Normandy from the same vantage point—the first one under a cloudy sky, and the second when the road was covered with snow.

DEGAS. PORTRAIT OF MANET STANDING. 1864-1866.
PRIVATE COLLECTION, PARIS.

DEGAS. GIRL WITH BINOCULARS. 1869-1872.
BURRELL COLLECTION, ART GALLERY AND MUSEUM, GLASGOW.

In the winter of 1864, Monet, Sisley, Bazille, and Renoir—the inseparables—were reunited in Paris. As far as the young Impressionists were concerned, their period of experimentation was over. They felt ready to submit their work to the jury of the 1865 Salon. Fantin-Latour decided to enter his *Toast,* Renoir his *Portrait of a Man* and *Summer Evening,* Monet his two views of the Seine estuary, and Manet his *Ecce Homo* and *Olympia.* "The crowd flocked around the putrescent *Olympia* and the revolting *Ecce Homo* of Monsieur Manet as if at the morgue," wrote Paul de Saint-Victor, and the praises of Baudelaire and Zola could not console Manet for the attacks heaped on him by Jules Claretie, who asked: "Who is this odalisque with the yellow stomach, this

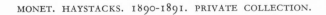

MONET. HAYSTACKS. 1890-1891. PRIVATE COLLECTION.

SISLEY. STUDY OF TREES. PENCIL.

wretched model picked up God knows where, who is supposed to be Olympia?" Even more dismaying to him was Courbet's comment: "Almost like the queen of spades in a deck of cards emerging from a bathtub." However, Monet won the approval of the painter and writer Zacharie Astruc, who wrote: "The creator of the most original and the subtlest seascape, the surest and most harmonious one to be exhibited in a long time. . . . Monsieur Monet, yesterday an unknown, has made a name for himself with this one painting." And Paul Mantz, the critic of the *Gazette des Beaux-Arts,* wrote: "His feeling for color harmonies and

Monet had found a house at Argenteuil. In order to be able to work in greater peace and, above all, in order to be in closer contact with his favorite element, water, he had built a studio boat modeled after Daubigny's famous "Botin" from which he loved to observe " the effects of light from dawn to twilight." There Monet entertained his friends, and Manet would often join them. Urged on by Berthe Morisot, Manet allowed himself to be converted to working in the open air, and on two occasions he set up his easel in front of the boat while Monet was working beside his wife. Manet greatly admired the character and talent of his friend and was impressed by his independence and his scorn of success.

The comparison between these two works, painted during the same year in the same place, demonstrates better than anything else the

MONET. THE STUDIO BOAT. C. 1874. RIJKSMUSEUM KRÖLLER-MÜLLER, OTTERLO.

MANET. CLAUDE MONET WORKING ON HIS BOAT. 1874.
BAYERISCHE STAATSGEMÄLDESAMMLUNGEN, MUNICH.

different temperaments of their creators. Manet, preoccupied with the pictorial qualities of his subject, used vivid colors and brilliant accents. What interested him above all was setting his figures in nature and achieving a unity between them and their surroundings. The whole layout of his composition reveals this concern. Monets, more restrained, more solitary, has a greater richness and vigor. The subject mattered little to him, it was merely a pretext for some new variation. He held to Manet's axiom that "Light is the main protagonist of a picture" even more obstinately than did Manet himself.

values, his fascinating over-all effects, his daring concepts, and his ability to capture the attention of the spectator—all these are qualities which Monsieur Monet already possesses to a high degree. Amid all the confusion of the exhibit, his *Seine Estuary* brought us to a sudden stop; we will never forget it. From now on, we are determined to follow the career of this upright painter of seascapes." But such enthusiastic comments were not symptomatic of the general reaction of the public. Not even Castagnary, who might have been expected to champion the work of his friends, paid more than passing attention to Manet and Monet. Dispirited and disappointed, Manet went off to Spain in search of fresh inspiration, while Monet decided to return to the Normandy coast, to be near Boudin and Courbet. There he buried himself in work, painting directly on white canvas in an attempt to develop a scale of color values "without regard to predetermined conditions."

BERTHE MORISOT AND EVA GONZALÈS JOIN THE GROUP. Youthful and slightly pugnacious, this nascent movement did not remain exclusively male. At the Louvre, Fantin had made the acquaintance of the Morisot sisters. There, under Corot's guidance, they were working on Pontoise and Auvers landscapes with a seriousness and conscientiousness not usually associated with well-to-do young ladies. Through Oudinot—their teacher and mentor, and himself a student of Corot—they had made the acquaintance of Daubigny, who also encouraged them in their work. Berthe Morisot had exhibited for the first time at the Salon of 1864. At the 1867 Salon, Manet, whose *Execution of Maximilian* had been rejected by the jury, was captivated by Berthe Morisot's *View of Paris*. A year later, in 1868, Fantin arranged a meeting between Manet and Berthe Morisot, and both artists made a lasting impression on each other. Berthe Morisot agreed to pose (with her mother acting as chaperone) for Manet's

MONET. FISHERMEN AT POISSY. 1882. FOGG MUSEUM OF ART, CAMBRIDGE, MASS.

The Balcony, which was then exhibited in the 1869 Salon. On the day of the opening, she wrote to her sister: "[Manet] begged me to go and look at his painting because he didn't dare go. I have never seen such an expressive face; he smiled anxiously and in rapid succession told me that his picture was very bad and that it was very successful. I find him most charming and like him immensely. As always, his paintings are reminiscent of a wild or not quite ripe fruit; I don't at all dislike them. In *The Balcony* I look strange rather than ugly; it seems that I have earned the epithet *femme fatale* among the curious." Soon thereafter, she graduated from model

Before Monet and Renoir, only Corot had been able to turn a landscape into that symphony of light and color in which the whole of nature—sky, earth, and man—is part of the joy of creation and the happiness of existence. Monet's specifically Impressionist style wrought few changes in the spirit of his work; all it did was to place more emphasis on something which was already apparent in certain landscapes of Corot. The scattering of reds among the greens was a strict application of the principle of color dissociation and of the law of complementary colors.

Renoir's picture shows the effects of the period when the two

MONET. A FIELD OF POPPIES. 1873. LOUVRE, PARIS.

RENOIR. ROAD CLIMBING THROUGH LONG GRASS. 1874. LOUVRE, PARIS.

painters worked together at Argenteuil during the year 1874. The subject is the same and it is similar in composition. But beyond these formal similarities there is a community of inspiration and the same attitude toward the motif; all the conditions are present for an art still too avant-garde *and personal to become the art of an epoch and a civilization. Nature, stripped of the sentimental and literary aura with which the Barbizon painters had surrounded it, regained a basic purity. Nothing was left of the picturesque or of local color; the only thing that mattered was the impression.*

SISLEY. RIVER BANK. PENCIL DRAWING.

to pupil, slightly resentful over having to share the approval of the master with Eva Gonzalès. But one thing remained certain: she never lost her gentleness, her intuition; she always remained aware of her limitations; she never tried to imitate Manet; she was completely feminine. The poet and critic Paul Valéry said: "Berthe Morisot was unique in that she lived her paintings and painted her life as if it were a natural and necessary function." It was she who persuaded Manet, the born city dweller, to paint in the open air. In 1872, she finally ceased to be a student, freeing herself from all that was imitative and inhibiting in her art. She achieved a soft,

PISSARRO. VILLAGE AMONG THE TREES. CABINET DES DESSINS, LOUVRE, PARIS.

delicate balance between color and light. In 1874, she married the master's brother, Eugène Manet, one of the men depicted in *Le Déjeuner sur l'Herbe*. This union brought her into even closer contact with Édouard. She stopped pursuing the laurels of the official Salon merely to satisfy the wishes of her parents, and devoted her days to painting subjects that reflected her own peaceful happiness—the faces of children, interiors, and landscapes. Together with her friends, she exhibited her work at Nadar's. Her art is evocative of Louis Watteau de Lille and of Gabriel de Saint-Aubin. Mallarmé said of her that " she had the same light touch

SISLEY.
BOAT DURING A FLOOD. 1876.
LOUVRE, PARIS.

Floods were a favorite subject with the Impressionists, and they were painted by Pissarro, Monet (in his Débâcles des Glaces), *and several times by Sisley himself. Floods were an ideal theme because they called not only for the dissolution of color but literally for the dissolution of the elements themselves where earth and sky merged. For Sisley the problem was a purely pictorial one, and he was careful never to introduce any facile, emotional interpretation. Precisely because he approached this sketch calmly and with restraint, because he was not concerned with an attractive composition, the effect is of an emotion far more subtle than that in the final picture,* Flood at Port-Marly *(also in the Louvre). Sisley's moderation and the poetic melancholy of his work reveal a temperament which was unquestionably refined, but one less vigorous than that of the other Impressionists.*

73

MANET. RUE DE BERNE. 1878. MUSÉE DES BEAUX-ARTS, BUDAPEST.

[as Monet, Sisley, and Renoir], wielding an eighteenth-century brush in the present." From 1884 onward, her work continued to show a heightened interest in line and bore the marks of a broader yet softer treatment. Light does not merely suffuse her paintings—it seems to penetrate and dissolve them.

Eva Gonzalès' creativity did not span as long a period as did Berthe Morisot's, nor was she as outstanding an artist, but she did follow a similar road. Manet taught her the importance of omission—to tackle the essential and forget embellishments. If some aspects of Impressionist painting remained alien to her, it was probably because Manet himself was not introduced to these until after his association with Berthe Morisot, and perhaps also because her husband, Henri Guérard, a collector and lover of Japanese prints, warned her against certain modern tendencies.

4

MANET, LEADER DESPITE HIMSELF

ON August 31, 1867, Baudelaire died at Neuilly after a long illness. Manet rushed back to Paris from Boulogne, where he had been vacationing, to say farewell to someone who, for almost ten years, had been a pillar of strength to him, almost his second self. Baudelaire had been a beacon for the generation of 1860; after his death Manet, having achieved a measure of fame by virtue of the scandalized reception accorded his *Déjeuner sur l'Herbe* and *Olympia,* became the new leader of this artistic movement, although he really was not cut out for the role, lacking both the necessary daring and the wish to lead. It almost seemed as if he took cover behind his paintings, whose purity and consummate perfection almost tended to obscure the man who created them. Though he may neither have desired nor fathomed it, revolution was inherent in his work. Fantin-Latour and Bazille, in their paintings of Manet and his friends, invariably show him in the traditional setting of a well-ordered, bourgeois home, not at all like the home of a painter. Manet, a Parisian and the son of a civil servant, remained closely tied to his own narrow circle and had little use for the café crowd with its slightly bizarre behavior. He shied away from too close an association with that young, noisy group who wanted to reform painting. Aside from a trip to Brazil and some brief time spent in Italy and in Spain, Manet hardly ever left Paris, the city that served him so well as a source of inspiration.

MANET. GEORGE MOORE AT THE CAFÉ DE LA NOUVELLE ATHÈNES. 1878.

Possessed of an astonishing visual sensibility, he was able to translate the sense of movement and myriad wonders of modern life into painting.   And he was able to accomplish this despite his training under Thomas Couture, despite the stable, bourgeois milieu in which he had grown up.   For nature had endowed him with a keen and astute sense of reality and with deep intuitive insight into the extraordinary qualities inherent in even the most sordid or common aspects of life.   This intuitive sense inevitably brought him into conflict with an academic tradition in which painting was meant to enhance, gloss over, or escape from reality.   When asked by a friend why there had been no progress in the drawing of hands, he replied: "Because hands are never in repose; they move."   In another context, he said: "In a figure, one must always

MANET. NANA. 1877. KUNSTHALLE, HAMBURG.

look for the highlights and the shadows; the rest will come by itself."

In a perceptive essay on the relationship between Baudelaire and Manet, Paul Valéry wrote: "There must be a deep kinship between a man able to write works like *Bénédiction, Tableaux Parisiens, Les Bijoux,* and *Le Vin des Chiffonniers* and a man able to paint

MANET. WOMAN BATHING. KOENIGS COLLECTION, BOYMANS MUSEUM, ROTTERDAM.

MANET. PORTRAIT OF BERTHE MORISOT. LITHOGRAPH.

pictures like *Christ with Angels, Olympia, Lola,* and *The Absinthe Drinker.* . . . Both came from the Parisian bourgeoisie, and their works show the same rare combination of refined elegance of taste and unique strength of execution. Furthermore, both men shun everything that does not spring from within themselves and their command of their respective media, and therein lies the *purity* of both painting and literature. The do not rely on *emotion,* they do not wish to proclaim *ideas* without prior intelligent and subtle organization of *feeling.* They pursue and attain the supreme goal of all art—magic—a word which I use here in its fullest sense." Manet's vitality, his thirst for life, undoubtedly saved him from getting the sort of official recognition which he seemed to want. Much has been made of the strange paradox of Manet, a good bourgeois who respected the established order, having become one of those embattled new painters, especially since he was fortunate enough not to have to live from his art. Above all, Manet had wanted to be accepted by the Salon. This may be difficult to understand today in an era when Salon has become the symbol of misjudgments and vapidity. But in 1861, when the jury accepted Manet's *Spanish Guitar Player,* he sought public confirmation of his choice of vocation—very understandable in the case of a young artist who wanted to justify himself before a reproachful family. He also saw in the Salon an opportunity to have his work compared with that of the established, older painters. And finally, from a purely material point of view, recognition by the Salon held out the promise of financial rewards. Both the public and the critics attached a great deal of importance to the medals and awards with which the state encouraged and rewarded its artists. Even Baudelaire, whose independence and integrity were beyond question, never discussed the rejected artists in his reviews of the Salon. Thus, for a protracted period, Manet made tentative approaches to the officials in charge. Toward this end, he maintained a tactful relationship with Couture, his teacher, while painters like Alfred Stevens and critics such as Wolff tried to add him to the ranks of officially sanctioned painters. But Manet's conciliatory efforts were all in vain. His *Déjeuner sur l'Herbe* (1863) created a scandal; society saw in his work the seed of revolution; it feared him as it feared every attempt to relate art to the

RENOIR. THE SWING. 1876. LOUVRE, PARIS.

RENOIR. STUDY FOR THE PORTRAIT OF JULIE MANET.
PRIVATE COLLECTION, PARIS.

reality of life. Indeed, society feared Manet even more than it feared Victor Hugo, despite Hugo's revolutionary ideas, since he, after all, confined himself to poetry.

MANET. THE SPRING. 1881. PRIVATE COLLECTION.

The Salons were not the entire world of painting. Young artists like Degas, Monet, Sisley, and Pissarro were eager to have Manet join their ranks. But Manet had misgivings about the role

CÉZANNE. SELF-PORTRAIT. C. 1876.
BAYERISCHE STAATSGEMÄLDESAMMLUNGEN, MUNICH.

"The human figure is the culmination of art," said Cézanne.   Conceived with an objectivity so perfect that all traces of psychology are excluded, this portrait achieves the sobriety of sculpture and attains the universality of those human types, severe and dignified, created by medieval sculptors.

they wanted him to play; he refused to become a prisoner of their principles. He never thought of himself as the creator of a new school of art. All he wanted was to be himself, to paint the way he had to paint. At times, Manet may have underestimated the significance and importance of his friends, and doubtless they gave him more—a bold spirit of adventure so alien to his nature, and, more important, an appreciation of his ideas—than he was able to give them. It was Berthe Morisot and Monet who persuaded him to paint in the open air—in sunlit fields and at the banks of the Seine—and the canvases he painted there bear a marked resemblance to the works of Morisot and Monet. He was always open-minded, receptive to outside influences; in 1874, he and his friends devoted themselves to open-air painting, and in 1877, he became deeply interested in naturalism. All these trends and influences are reflected in his work, but none diverted him from the road that was his very own—the simple harmony of light and dark shades.

The difference in background between Manet and his friends hardly contributed toward close relationships. Degas' biting cynicism contrasted sharply with Manet's jovial urbanity. It is difficult to picture these two sitting side by side in the Café de la Nouvelle Athènes: Édouard, fashionable, well-groomed, with soft, almost feminine hands; Edgar, unkempt, tall, and abrupt. Degas was not given to sparing his friend: "Manet is desperate because he is unable to paint atrocious pictures like Duran's, because he does not get acclaim and medals. He is an artist by compulsion, not by inclination. He is a galley slave chained to his oars." Sisley, Renoir, and Pissarro also did not feel too much at ease in Manet's rather elegant apartment. They were hesitant about coming to the intimate Thursday-night gatherings which were attended by men like Zola, Astruc, Théodore Duret, Clemenceau, and Antonin Proust; they preferred the informality of the Café Guerbois. Berthe Morisot, however, did not hesitate to install herself in Manet's studio, and by marrying Manet's brother, she lent respectability to an artistic relationship which might have seemed somewhat equivocal in so bourgeois a setting.

Even though Manet sometimes failed to heed the demands made on him by this group of friends, he never failed to help when help was urgently needed. With generosity and selflessness he came to the aid of his less fortunate colleagues, regardless of the artistic content of their work. Although he did not participate in the first exhibition the group held in 1874, the public disapproval accorded the works exhibited was extended to him also. However, he tried to change the climate of opinion, to conciliate the art critics and art dealers, by intervening with the very influential M. Wolff of *Le Figaro*.

In the normal course of events, Manet would have succeeded his father in his post at the Ministry of Justice or, at worst, would have become a successful traditional painter. But instead, he became a revolutionary despite himself, merely because he strove to express faithfully what he saw. In an era of banality, this intrepid search for truth forced him to become an outsider. Thus Manet, an errant classicist amidst a group of young barbarians, became the leader of a school, even came to be considered the founder of Impressionism. But in truth he was simply the last link in a tradition of painting—Chardin, Watteau, Corot, Manet. Prior to his *Olympia* he was only the excellent "bad" pupil of Couture. He was too intelligent and too conscientious to reject a tradition which weighed on him heavily, but whose necessity he recognized. He would have liked to have recreated the illusion of volume and perspective as did all painters of "nice" pictures, but instead his paintings became large planes, strong in color, devoid of halftones and finely modulated shadings, and because all geometric representations of space were repugnant to him, his pictures were composed like bas-reliefs. His inner vision was stronger than he.

PISSARRO. WOMAN EMPTYING A WHEELBARROW. ETCHING.

It was the sincere belief of Couture that he would be able to achieve a synthesis between David's classicism and Courbet's sensuous realism, and Manet struggled through six long years of this sort of instruction, the foredoomed struggle of a man who lacked the imagination and inventiveness to paint something he

PISSARRO.
THE RED ROOFS. 1877.
LOUVRE, PARIS.

Pissarro, who lived at Pontoise, loved the fields and the orchards, the soft light and the quiet peace of the Vexin countryside, and it was there that he reached his full artistic maturity. In the foreground of this painting the trees cast their shadows over the ground ; through the network of branches a number of brightly colored roofs stand out against the background of fields. Thus dissociated, the elements of the landscape are recreated in a single equal vibration. Nevertheless, Pissarro never used a landscape as a pretext for dazzling the spectator. "One must," he said, "be humble in front of nature. The desire to interpret must not make one lose intimate, direct contact with it."

89

cannot feel and see.   Distraught over his inability to follow the dictates of abstract rules which he had been taught to regard as the perpetuation of genuine tradition, Manet sought an answer to his problem among the old masters, particularly of the Spanish school. But even in those of his works influenced by Velasquez, Ribera, and Goya—for example, *The Spanish Guitar Player* (1860), *Portrait of Baudelaire's Mistress,* and *The Old Musician* (1862)—he experimented with strong tonal contrasts, omitting softening halftones.   These apparent errors and deficiencies soon led him to abandon the goal he had set himself, and, leaving the confines of the studio, he set out to capture the quality of light.   That he did not succeed in this at once is evident in such early paintings as *Déjeuner sur l'Herbe,* which is touching in its hesitancy and disregard for the subject. The scandalized reception of this canvas did not bother Manet.   He was concerned solely with achieving the desired effect—silence and light.   The storm which then greeted the showing of his *Olympia* in the Salon of 1865 helped to bring about his final breach with the established schools.   The public, not knowing or not caring to know the tradition of Titian and Goya which had inspired Manet, felt repelled not so much by the indecency of the subject as by the style of painting.   Undogmatic and unfettered by intellectualization, driven by an inner force beyond his control, Manet revolutionized art.   He achieved his vision: to strip art of all preconceived notions, to paint truthfully rather than prettily.

Neither Manet nor his circle of Impressionist friends was aware of the importance of his message.   And in fact, his pursuit of the fleeting impression cannot easily be reconciled with his classical temperament.   Nonetheless, he became the creator of *Olympia* and *The Flutist,* superb paintings that capture all the hard, frank, relentless impact of light.

Standing on the borderline between two worlds, between two epochs, Manet represented the summation of the long-reigning

RENOIR. THE ORANGE-SELLER. SANGUINE. PRIVATE COLLECTION.

studio tradition, and at the same time he was the herald of a future
of continual creativity, joy, and love.   But he was unaware
that he was to become the precursor of a new way of experiencing

RENOIR. THE END OF THE LUNCH. 1879.
STÄDELSCHES KUNSTINSTITUT, FRANKFURT.

This picture, redolent with a warm, healthy, and vibrant sensuality, was painted under the arbor of Olivier's restaurant in Montmartre ; in it, Renoir has grouped together the actress Ellen Andrée (who posed for Degas' Absinthe), the son of a Nantes shipowner, and Marguerite, his current model.

Renoir's official break with the Impressionists came in the years 1879-1880. In leaving them, he said: "Out of doors one has a far greater variety of light than the light of the studio, which is always the same, but, precisely because of this, you are so taken up with the light out of doors that you have no time to concern yourself with composition; then again, out of doors, you can't see what you are doing. . . . When painting from nature, the painter reaches the stage of seeking only after the effect, of no longer paying any attention to composition, and he rapidly becomes monotonous." With these words Renoir felt that he was denying both a system and the friendships to which, for all that, his vision remained faithful.

RENOIR. THE SEINE AT ASNIÈRES. C. 1879. LADY ABERCONWAY COLLECTION, LONDON.

reality. He opened up vistas which he himself did not know existed, and men whom he never would have numbered among his friends were to take up his message. Painters are not responsible for that which they create. It does not belong to them, and it is frequently greater than they are. Posterity makes it its own and revels in it. Manet's work was so full of problems and had so many hidden facets that it was not at all surprising for artists in search of a leader to choose him for their own. Yet, at the same time, the unorthodoxy of his work precluded its annexation by any given school. The essence of his work was elusive and indefinable, and Manet himself was never able to put it into words. If the Cubists consider Ingres their precursor, then the Fauves may lay claim to Manet, who, according to Matisse, "was the first who translated his emotions directly, thus giving free rein to instinct."

DEGAS. HORSE AND JOCKEY. COLLECTION KOENIGS,
BOYMANS MUSEUM, ROTTERDAM.

5

DEGAS,
THE CLASSICIST OF IMPRESSIONISM

DEGAS had much in common with Manet. They were the same age—the oldest members of their group—and they had already found their styles while the others were still dreaming of revolutionizing painting. Despite their independence, both admitted to emotional ties to the classical tradition and, both in their own way, were aristocrats. Manet liked to please and wanted to be loved; Degas' attraction lay in his distinguished reserve, his politeness, his disdain for convention, his wit. A keen observer, Degas was not satisfied to accept the outer appearance of things; he tested and analyzed, not without irony and never without that "cold fever" of which Huysmans spoke. His self-portrait, painted in 1855, shows him with serious and penetrating gaze, with a sensual yet bitter mouth. Edgar De Gas, the son of a wealthy, aristocratic Italian father and an American mother, had received a good, classical education, and it was the hope of his parents that he would enter his father's banking business. But his independent wealth permitted him to follow his inclination and enroll in an art school. However, the Louvre, not the art school, became his true teacher. He spent endless hours there, copying, studying, and copying. Poussin was a revelation, and through him he was to discover Italy. He steered clear of all the intrigues of the world of art. All he wanted was solitude in which to find himself.

After his return to Paris in 1860, he no longer was a novice.

DEGAS. JOCKEYS IN THE RAIN. C. 1881.
BURRELL COLLECTION, ART GALLERY AND MUSEUM, GLASGOW.

Degas' artistic development took place on the fringe of Impression-ism.   With his innate love of classicism, he was not the man to be tied down by any one system.   Though a misanthrope and a lover of solitude, he had to be surrounded by movement, for in the movement of things and people he found consolation.   Like an entomologist pinning down his butterflies, Degas pinpointed the rider, the dancer, the objects that delighted him.   He was, in fact, less a painter of the moment than of the momentary.   Lautrec shared his tastes, but, although an equally frank analyst, he retained a warm sympathy for his subjects.   Anglophilia had given rise to a vogue for horse-racing, and specialized painters like Carle Vernet and Eugène Lamy had created their own genre which exalted the nobility of the thorough-bred and its rider.   For Degas, as for Lautrec, the problem was a different one.   Undoubtedy their education and background made them responsive to the elegance and breeding of the horses and the agility of the jockeys ; but it was the event itself and the setting in the open air which most aroused their enthusiasm.

TOULOUSE-LAUTREC. JOCKEY GOING TO THE POST. 1899.
LITHOGRAPH.

DEGAS. THREE DANCERS. CHARCOAL AND PASTEL. 1879.
MRS. J. WATSON WEBB COLLECTION, NEW YORK.

He was an established craftsman, sure of himself. His choice of
subjects remained classical; even Ingres would not have disagreed
with them. But he imbued his subjects with an unconventional
power of observation which found its natural expression in themes
from everyday life. At about this period of his career, he met
Manet at the Louvre. Manet, overwhelmed by the masterful
quality of a copy Degas was making at the museum, made the first
move. Also, he probably sensed in Degas the sort of elegance
that differentiated both these men from the usual run of sorry

dabblers who frequented the museum. The two men became
friends, and Manet, having already gained some renown and
recognition, felt free to advise Degas to stop painting "grandiose"

DEGAS. TWO DANCERS IN TIGHTS. 1892-1895.
DURAND-RUEL COLLECTION, PARIS.

RENOIR. DANCING IN THE COUNTRY. 1883. DRAWING.

RENOIR. BATHER. 1881. SIR KENNETH CLARK COLLECTION, LONDON.

canvases, to rid himself of all academic ballast, to go out and observe the life around him. But Degas' naturalism was only a temporary concession to the new ideology; basically a classicist, he preferred elegant · subjects—especially racing and the world of ballet. Despite his involvement with the Impressionist movement, with its fights and its experiments, he retained a certain upper-class, noncommittal aloofness. He always remained a spectator rather than a participant, victimized by his prejudices, shy, afraid of displays of emotion, an outsider. Keenly analytical, he was the only one among his contemporaries who knew how to capture an instantaneous vision without sacrificing truth. Yet, Degas' truth was not without plan or aim; its trace of irony seemed designed to screen his sensitivity. Was it accidental that his women always are seen to their least advantage, with fatigue in their eyes—exhausted, heavy-limbed dancers, cleaning-women hardly able to drag their heavy pails around? Was this denial of lyricism an expression of cynicism, or was it an expression of a nonconformity which rejected feminine beauty along with convention? Degas was a lonely man who hated loneliness; he needed "the movement of people and things which diverts and consoles. If the leaves never moved, how sad the trees would be, and we with them." But this sort of candid confession was in stark contradiction—and this was the great conflict in Degas' life—to the guiding principle he laid down for himself: "One must submit to rigid discipline." Thus, he was tied and imprisoned by his own principles. Degas was a virtuoso, but primarily he seemed to be a dissatisfied artist seeking new methods, eager for new, rare approaches. In this search, he utilized every tool at his disposal—charcoal, pastels, pencil, lithography, etching needle, brush, even the sculptor's chisel. His art, daring and unusual, conveyed movement, it had a theatrical quality, and through it he was able to identify himself with his subjects.

6

A WAR DISRUPTS THE GROUP

THE carefree, happy life of this young, vital group—whose fervor and creativity enabled them to withstand the snubs of officialdom, the ignorance and stupidity of the public, and the poverty which was the lot of most of them—came to a sudden end with the outbreak of the Franco-Prussian War in 1870. The war scattered them: Manet, Degas, Bazille, and Renoir joined various branches of military service; Monet and Pissarro went to England; Cézanne sought refuge in the country. Pissarro and Monet, sitting out the war in London, made the acquaintance of another refugee, the art-dealer Durand-Ruel, who was to become a firm supporter and promoter of this new group of artists. After the siege of Paris, and then the Commune with its attendant terror, the Impressionists reassembled in Paris. They all came back, all but Bazille—the most charming, most beloved member of the circle—who had died in action soon after the outbreak of the war.

NEW INFLUENCES. War and exile seemed to have matured many of these young men. The stay in London had wrought significant changes in the lives of Monet and Pissarro. It brought them closer to the school of English landscape painters, and it was the beginning of their association with Durand-Ruel, who, following the dictates of his own taste, stood ready to sacrifice his reputation and his wealth to help the artists he admired. At the outbreak

MANET. LE BAR AUX FOLIES-BERGÈRE. 1882.
COURTAULD INSTITUTE, LONDON.

104

"*When I returned to Paris in January 1882, my first visit was to Manet.* He was then painting Le Bar aux Folies-Bergère *and the model, a pretty girl, was posing behind a table laden with bottles and food.* . . . *Although he used models for his pictures, Manet was no copyist of nature ; I particularly noticed his masterful simplifications. The head of the woman was clearly shaped, but this quality was not obtained by an imitation of nature. Everything was re-modeled: the tones were brighter, the colors more vivid, the values closer together. The result was a gentle, light harmony.* . . . *Manet interrupted his work and sat with me on the divan. He talked with me and said: 'Concision in art is both necessary and elegant. The concise man makes one think ; the talkative man irritates.* . . . *In a figure, look for the highlights and the deepest shadows ; the rest will come naturally ; often it is very little. Also, train your memory ; for nature will never give you more than indications.'*" (*From an article by Jeanniot published in* La Grande Revue *of August, 1907.*) *The picture met with considerable success in the Salon of 1882 and resulted in Manet being awarded the Legion of Honor he so coveted.*

of the war, Durand-Ruel left his shop at the Rue Laffitte, where he had exhibited the Barbizon painters, and moved to New Bond Street in London. Daubigny followed him to London, and it was he who introduced him to Monet and Pissarro. Durand-Ruel bought some of their canvases and lent them material assistance. Had he done nothing else, he would deserve the gratitude of posterity, for Victorian gentry displayed little interest in a school of painting so devoid of intellectual pretension, so far removed from any ideal of beauty, so full of sensuality. As far as French art was concerned, the only painters accepted in England were Gérôme and Rosa Bonheur. England was acquainted neither with Corot nor any of the other great figures of the preceding twenty-five years. Monet, Pissarro, and Sisley—strengthened by Durand-Ruel's support—were not to be dismayed by the lack of appreciation of London art circles. Captivated with countryside and suburbs of London, with the effects of fog, snow, and spring sunshine, they worked hard. They visited museums, delighting in the portraits and water colors of Turner and Constable, admiring the canvases of Old Crome, Gainsborough, Lawrence, and Reynolds. But the landscape painters, these masters of light and fleeting impressions, affected them most, and of these, Turner was the greatest revelation. The magic of his delicate colors electrified them; they tried to analyze his technique, to discover the secret of his art. His snow and ice scenes, in particular, left an indelible impression on them. Signac, in his *From Delacroix to Neo-Impressionism,* wrote: "They were astonished at his ability to recreate the whiteness of snow, something they themselves with their broad brush strokes had not been able to achieve. And they realized that this wonderful effect could not be achieved with a uniform white, but only through numerous closely applied dots in a variety of colors which, seen from a distance, merged to give the desired effect." This lesson was never forgotten by them.

7

THEORIES AND PRACTICES
OF IMPRESSIONISM

THOSE who thought that the creation of the Third Republic would change old, established institutions soon were to learn otherwise. Revolutionary artists remained suspect—and the Salon jury adamant. It rejected Renoir's *Parisian Women Dressed as Algerians,* a painting strongly influenced by Delacroix, and Manet, whose *Le Bon Bock* met with resounding success in 1873, was refused another medal highly coveted by him. But the other members of the group, aware of the unchanged climate of the Salon, did not even bother to submit entries. Instead, they exhibited with their friend Durand-Ruel, who showed their work in London, in New York, and in his new Paris gallery in the Rue Le Peletier. Thus the break with art officialdom became complete, and no opportunistic considerations would ever again deter any of them from following their own way. Up to that time, the friendly spirit of competition which had animated the group had served as a substitute for theory. True, all of them were enthusiastic admirers of Delacroix, Courbet, Manet, and Corot, but now they had to break away, to follow their own instinctive feeling for light. In translating the purity and brilliance of their vision, they eliminated every trace of earth color, burnt sienna, and black from their palettes; they sought to achieve warm grays, blues, greens, and violets, using only pure colors, applying them in stabbing dots. The direct, empirical study of

RENOIR. GIRL AGAINST A BLUE BACKGROUND. 1882.
PRIVATE COLLECTION, PARIS.

*A softness of form, a smooth, almost enameled treatment and pearly tones—
Renoir was undoubtedly trying to depict "skin which does not repel light,"
but that is not enough to make a portrait. One gets the feeling that
around 1880-1883, the artist had exhausted the resources of Impressionism
and had arrived at a dead end. "I knew neither how to paint nor how to
draw," he confessed. It was then that he decided to go to Italy and study
the masters of the Renaissance.*

the effect of light on form had become their stated objective, and their naturalism developed into a search for the accurate and precise depiction of pure sensation. The almost literal translation of the subject was being replaced by a new world of color, values, and form—the world of Impressionism. These painters who had rejected the sterility of official schools fell victim to scientific methods. Although their artistic instinct was stronger than all formulas, the lure of science was at times strong enough to wreak havoc with style, to give their art a contrived quality.

Every primary color becomes intensified when brought in contact with another primary color. If blue and red are juxtaposed closely, they will appear from a distance to be more vividly violet than either of the primary colors. Leonardo had already held that the shadow cast by a man on a white wall appears blue, and Rubens in his treatise *On Colors* had stated that "in a picture, shadow and light should not cover more than one-third of the canvas; two-thirds should be reserved for half tones." By using entirely different color for half tones in the transition between light and shadow, Fragonard and Delacroix had discovered a new luminosity. Thus, the Impressionists did not really discover anything new. They merely found a new relationship to light. Edmond Duranty, the publisher of *Réalisme* and friend to the group, wrote: "They discovered that full light robs tones of color, that the purity of sunlight reflected by objects reimbues the objects with a luminous unity which blends the seven spectral rays of the prism into the one colorless beam which is light. Intuitive step by intuitive step, they succeeded in dissolving sunlight into individual rays, into its elements, and then in reinvesting it with unity through the harmony of the spectral colors which they applied to their canvases." This perception led the Impressionists to a shift in emphasis—from the observation of the contours of light to capturing the changed appearance of the subject under various light

RENOIR. STUDY FOR "THE BATHERS." PRIVATE COLLECTION, U.S.A.

conditions, resulting in the dissolution of form, in the creation of a world which was but a reflection of a reflection in which man no longer existed. Such an approach is necessarily limited, since it is confined to a fleeting instance, to the changing face of a landscape, and not to the face of man. Under the pretext of striving toward an objective, the scientific analysis of optical effects, Impressionism led to a passionate recreation of a given moment in nature. The motif became of little or no importance.

MONET, THE LEADING EXPONENT. Monet was the leading exponent of this development, and in his *Haystacks* (1891-1892), *Poplars* (1890-1892), *Cathedrals* (1893-1894), and *Water*

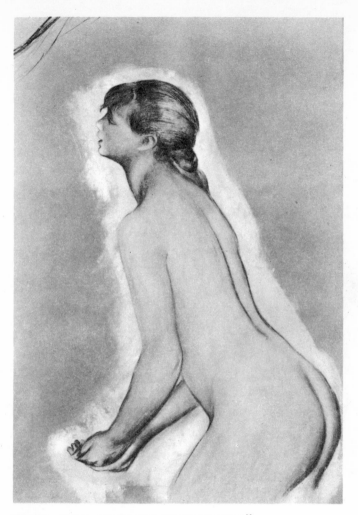

RENOIR. NUDE. STUDY FOR "THE BATHERS."
ART INSTITUTE, CHICAGO.

Lilies (1904) series, he gave expression to this non-objective recreation of the moment.   Later in his life, Monet denied having been a theoretician, and he even came close to renouncing the friendly ties which had bound him to the other members of the

MORISOT. THE TERRACE AT MEUDON. 1884. ART INSTITUTE, CHICAGO.

Men like to believe that creative talent is their private domain and that paintings by women lack originality, that they are either charmingly or slavishly imitative. But eighteenth-century painting—which one tends to classify as feminine—was the work of men. This is the eternal misunderstanding. It would be truer to say that women do not borrow from men but that they do refer to them ; for example, Morisot to Manet and Cassatt to Degas. But there is a world in which the women excel—in depicting maternity and childhood. "She did not try to ecape from herself, to turn herself from something artificial and false," wrote Louis Rouart of Berthe Morisot. "All simplicity and naturalness, she remained a woman." And this very simplicity gives even the most minor of her works a charm which is neither affected nor unfeeling.

As for Mary Cassatt, the admiration that Degas had for her—and he was niggardly with compliments—would be sufficient justification for her fame, even if she had not done so much on behalf of Impressionist painting in the United States. These two delightful women occupied a special niche in the Impressionist movement, and their names are deservedly recorded in the history of art.

CASSATT. THE LITTLE SISTERS. 1885. ART GALLERY AND MUSEUM, GLASGOW.

group: He wrote: "I have always had a horror of theory . . . the only merit I have is that of painting from nature, of trying to convey my impressions of the most fleeting effects, and I regret having become the one for whom a group, most of whose members had nothing of the Impressionist in them, was named." If the secret of Monet's work had consisted solely in a skillful juggling of colors, a rapid notation of a momentary effect, then indeed his dangerous experiment would have been nothing but a new academic formula. But a method of painting is far important than the sensitivity of the painter, and if Monet's work can be said to have been motivated by an inner necessity, it was one which conformed to the international taste of his time—the mist which seems to dissolve form, a dreamlike lyricism, inspired by England—but one which cannot be divorced from his profound feeling for a world in movement, a cosmic reality in which the miraculous and the enchanting are more real than nature itself. Shelley's poem "The Sensitive Plant," written a century earlier, almost reads like a description of Monet's water lilies in the garden at Giverny:

> *And on the stream whose inconstant bosom*
> *Was pranked, under boughs of embowering blossom,*
> *With golden and green light, slanting through*
> *Their heaven of many a tangled hue.*
>
> *Broad water-lilies lay tremulously,*
> *And starry river-buds glimmered by,*
> *And around them the soft stream did glide and dance*
> *With a motion of sweet sound and radiance.*

Reflection, the mere suggestion of the object that renders it far more seductive than reality itself, and the resultant disembodiment of the concrete world surrounding us—these were Monet's contributions to painting.

8

THE BAPTISM OF THE MOVEMENT

THE dissolution of form and the persistent search for tonal values were almost symbolic of the approaching parting of the ways of the Impressionists. Together they had discovered the power of light—their credo—but, paradoxically, at the time the movement was baptized, the group was on the verge of breaking up. Each of the artists stood ready to follow his own vision separately.

THE FIRST IMPRESSIONIST EXHIBITION. The group held its first joint exhibition in 1874 in the studio of the photographer Nadar. In order to avoid any tendentious interpretation of their aims, they chose as neutral a name for themselves as possible— *Société Anonyme Coopérative d'Artistes, Peintres, Sculpteurs, Graveurs, etc.* But the paradox of history was to intervene. Monet, equally intent on finding neutral titles for his paintings, had labeled one of them *Impression, Sunrise,* which became the heading of a highly critical review of the exhibition published in *Charivari.* Thus, the term Impressionism became the name and the program of this group of artists. There were thirty of them, and perhaps at this point one should name these courageous artists who were ready to brave public ridicule and exhibit jointly with those previously rejected by the Salon. They were: Astruc, Attendu, Béliard, Boudin, Bracquemond, Brandon, Bureau, Cals, Cézanne, Colin, Degas, Desbras, Guillaumin, Latouche, Lepic, Lépine,

SEURAT. LA PROMENEUSE AU SINGE.
STUDY FOR "LA GRANDE JATTE." 1885.
SMITH COLLEGE MUSEUM OF ART, NORTHAMPTON, MASS.

Levert, Meyer, De Molins, Monet, Berthe Morisot, Mulot-Durivage, De Nittis, A. Ottin, L. A. Ottin, Pissarro, Renoir, Robert, Rouart, and Sisley. Twelve years later, at their last exhibit in 1886, there were only five: Degas, Guillaumin, Berthe Morisot, Pissarro, and Rouart.

Pissarro was the only artist represented in all of the eight exhibitions sponsored by the Impressionists. This loyalty to his friends and the strength of his convictions were characteristic of Pissarro, and perhaps he may therefore be considered the ideal Impressionist. Simple and unpretentious, he may have lacked the creative ability and boldness of a Monet; his interpretation of nature is calmer, more prosaic, more modest, but his style is more resolute. Perhaps

SEURAT. THE ISLAND OF LA GRANDE JATTE. 1884-1885. PRIVATE COLLECTION, U.S.A.

Pissarro was in such need of friendship because he was lonely after leaving his native Saint Thomas in the Danish Antilles for Paris. The friends made in the studios—these were his new family to whom he remained faithful. There was something of

CÉZANNE. MONT
SAINTE-VICTOIRE. 1885-1887.
METROPOLITAN MUSEUM
OF ART, NEW YORK.

"Allow me to repeat what I have already said to you here: treat nature in terms of the cylinder, the sphere, and the cone; put the whole into the proper perspective so that each side of an object or a plane converges toward some central point. Lines parallel to the horizon give breadth . . . lines perpendicular to this horizon give depth. But, for us, nature consists more in depth than in surface, hence the need to introduce into our vibrations of light, represented by reds and yellows, enough bluish tints to give the feeling of air." From a letter of Cézanne to Émile Bernard.

the prophet about Pissarro, "the modest colossus." His friends called him "Moses bearing the tablets of the law" when they saw him coming with his portfolio under his arm. When he settled in Pontoise in 1872, he gathered his old friends of the Académie Suisse around him: Guillaumin, Cézanne, and a small group of enthusiastic novices. There he taught them, but he was neither surprised nor offended when they later went their own ways. He never felt himself to be the father-confessor. With inborn grace and an exalted sense of obligation as the oldest member of the group, he stood by the younger men, supporting them in their experiments without imposing his own conceptions on them. On the contrary, when he helped Cézanne find himself, he became influenced by Cézanne and from him he acquired his profound

CÉZANNE. LANDSCAPE. 1880-1885. ART INSTITUTE, CHICAGO.

PISSARRO. PORTRAIT OF CÉZANNE. LOUVRE, PARIS.

feeling for the relation between color and form. Some years later, influenced by the theories of the young Seurat, he became a temporary adherent of Neo-Impressionism. Cézanne said of him: "Pissarro was like a father. He is a man to whom one can turn for advice; he is something like God."

Firmly convinced of the significance of Impressionism, Pissarro became its defender and apostle. "In nature, look for that which expresses your own temperament; in a motif, form and color, not the drawing, are of primary importance. . . . Precision in drawing is dry and detracts from the over-all impression; it destroys all emotion.   Precision of contour is not important; a brush stroke of the right value and color should produce the final work. The most difficult problem is not that of detail of contour but the reproduction of content.   One must paint the essential characteristics of objects, to try to convey them with any means whatsoever without worrying about technique.   In painting, you must choose your subject, you must see what is to the right and to the left of it, and then you must work on the whole simultaneously. . . . Observe the perfection of the atmosphere from foreground to the horizon, observe the reflection of the sky and of foliage.   Don't hesitate to apply color, then refine your work little by little.   Don't adhere to rules and principles.   Paint what you see and feel— boldly, without hesitation, for it is best not to lose your first impression.   One cannot be timid in the face of nature; one must dare to make mistakes.   There can be but one teacher—nature. She must always be consulted."   This was the credo of the perfect Impressionist.   Pissarro may have been unsuccessful in completely converting Cézanne to his method, but he was able to teach him the sort of discipline acquired through the observation of nature, as well as a feeling for structure.   "We were always together," wrote Pissarro, "but it cannot be denied that each of us retained the only thing that really matters—our individual emotion."   The one—Pissarro—covered his canvas with stabbing, powerful brush strokes; the other with broad flat planes.   A peasant who once watched them paint the identical subject commented that "M. Pissarro stabbed while he worked, and M. Cézanne daubed."   Pissarro's *Hermitage at Pontoise* and Cézanne's *The House of the Hanged Man,* both painted in 1873, are testimony to their shared experience.

Sisley never became an intimate member of the group, but he

CÉZANNE. VIEW OF L'ESTAQUE. C. 1885. R. A. BUTLER COLLECTION, LONDON.

followed its work and activities closely. Like Pissarro and
Cézanne, he, too, set up his easel out of doors—in Pontoise, Marly,
Louveciennes, and Bougival. He was too shy, too well-bred,
too sensitive to become an active participant in the great Impressionist adventure. Despite his talent, despite the fact that he may
even be considered more typical an Impressionist than Pissarro,
he remained a minor though pleasant artist among the giants of
the movement. His reserve prevented him from joining in the
stormy, intense life of the Studio Gleyre group, yet as long as his
financial position permitted, he did accompany his friends on their
trips to Fontainebleau and along the banks of the Seine. When,
after the death of his father in 1870, he lost his independent income,
he gradually broke away from the group, retreating to the solitude
of Louveciennes and Moret. He sought refuge in the silence of

VAN GOGH. THE GARDENS OF THE TUILERIES.
V. W. VAN GOGH COLLECTION, LAREN.

GOGH. THE TERRACE IN THE TUILERIES. 1886. V. W. VAN GOGH COLLECTION, LAREN.

nature, creating a series of limpid, airy paintings. His delicate, sensitive technique embodied an almost feminine melancholy grace. Neither poverty nor lack of understanding for his art ever changed him; his style retained its elegance and refinement, and these qualities undoubtedly accounted for the success his work enjoyed with collectors—after his death. While he lived, his work was rejected along with that of his colleagues.

In 1874—the same year in which the Salon exhibited Bouguereau's *Nymphs and Satyr,* the epitome of all the hollowness and falseness of the academic tradition—Renoir exhibited at Nadar's his *Loge,* a testimony to the powerful artistic temperament of this painter. One can almost hear in his painting the discordant tones

VAN GOGH. LE MOULIN DE LA GALETTE. 1886.
ART GALLERY AND MUSEUM, GLASGOW.

In 1886, Van Gogh arrived in Paris. Pissarro, Signac, Gauguin, and Émile Bernard took him under their wing and gave him advice. "We painted the river banks," relates Signac, "we lunched in the taverns and

VAN GOGH. MONTMARTRE: THE STREET LAMPS. 1886.
ART INSTITUTE, CHICAGO.

walked into Paris. . . . Van Gogh, wearing blue workingmen's overalls, had daubed little splashes of color on his sleeves." Vincent's somber palette became lighter. He grew bolder and began to adopt vigorous brushstrokes.

of the violins being tuned amid the buzz of conversation, and the soft glow of the pearls around the throat of a young woman seems to hold forth the promise of an evening of pleasure.   The glitter of society, the brilliance of the jewels worn by the women undoubtedly appealed to Renoir's sense of beauty, yet at the same time the emptiness of that mode of life left him dissatisfied.   He was compelled by instinct to seek after absolute, permanent values. Though by no means an intellectual, he respected and loved the works of the old masters.   He believed that a painter had to paint in the idiom of his era, but he also believed that a study of the old masters could give the artist a feeling for painting which he could not gain by the study of nature alone.   He wanted to paint freely, not to either follow a style or create one.   He was famous for his witty remarks, revealing a temperament to which all dogma and all formulas were alien: "If God had not created breasts, I would not have become a painter," he once said, and also: "I am a painter, not a chemist."   His instinct for truth and his passionate love of color led him to Rubens, to Fragonard and Delacroix, and ultimately to Monet.   But once he suspected that the experiments of his friends were in danger of becoming a system, he realized that he had arrived at an impasse, and with this realization came the desire to break through the circle which threatened to close him in.   Seen from this perspective, his *Loge* and *Moulin de la Galette* represent Renoir at the height of orthodox Impressionism.   Yet, these paintings already heralded a new Renoir, one who sought for truth and certainty; and the only inner certainty he knew was that of the senses.   He felt repelled by reason and doctrine, by the search for the absolute.   And thus he came to a parting of the ways with Monet's Impressionism, which he considered a convention, the representation of an abstract world which had no room for the human factor.   He returned to the eighteenth century and attempted to create a sort of synthesis between Impressionism and the

RENOIR. BATHER SEEN FROM THE BACK. ALBERTINA, VIENNA.

enchanted world of Watteau. His doubts about the validity of much of Impressionist theory were strengthened during a trip to Italy in 1881. There he discovered Raphael, who, he said, "did not seek the impossible." "In 1883," he said, "there came some-

VAN GOGH. VIEW FROM VINCENT'S ROOM, RUE LEPIC. 1887.
V. W. VAN GOGH COLLECTION, LAREN.

TOULOUSE-LAUTREC. PORTRAIT OF SUZANNE VALADON. 1885.
NY CARLSBERG GLYPTOTEK, COPENHAGEN.

*Attracted by everything out of the ordinary, Toulouse-Lautrec was
bound to be delighted with the vigorous temperament of Degas'
model, Suzanne Valadon. Being more of a draughtsman than a
painter, his oil paintings have the quality of pastel drawings.*

thing like a break in my work." After that, he devoted much of his time to drawing, an aspect of art which all the other Impressionists had neglected in their attempt to preserve the primary emotion of painting.

His style became influenced by Boucher and Fragonard; his search for perfection drew him to Ingres as well as to Raphael; he was filled with admiration for the sureness and decisiveness of Japanese art. When Renoir finally arrived at a synthesis of all these seemingly contradictory schools, achieving a balance of observation, color, and form, he also recovered the richness of his palette. He achieved a simplicity which added to the breadth of his vision, the fullness of his forms, the richness of his colors. His women—the snub-nosed, childish, sensuous, naïve, naughty models from Montmartre and the peasant girls from Essoyes and Cagnes— these individual, universal beauties symbolized the "intimate caress of light created by Renoir." In his use of light, he never ceased to be an Impressionist.

DEGAS. WASHERWOMEN. 1892-1895. PRIVATE COLLECTION.

9

FOUR GIANTS
OF POST-IMPRESSIONISM

ART critics and art historians alike easily conform to habit. Thus, Impressionism has come to be equated with all French painting toward the end of the nineteenth century, though it represented only a small part of the creative output of that period. Impressionism showed the way to new approaches and bold experiments, and consequently it became fashionable to identify all contemporary developments with this particular movement, however unrelated or alien they might be.

From the very beginning, Impressionism contained within itself the seeds of its decline, the basic contradiction between an effective, rational technique—the logically perfect expression of the scientific spirit—and an art form searching for the immediate, spontaneous contact with the world around it which appeals to the instinct and rejects all method. The Impressionist revolution, fought under the banner of positivism, wished to free painting of everything which was not a simple reproduction of nature ; it wished to capture the purity of the image as perceived by the eye. Thus, the subject became secondary, a pretext for painting for its own sake. By reducing the palette to the primary colors, Impressionism freed the artist from the chains of artificiality and super-refinement.

Impressionism gave to artists a glimpse of the "promised land" in the emancipation of color and form. In its narrowest sense, it lasted only a few years. But the spirit of adventure and search which had inspired the Impressionists was reincarnated in the works of Cézanne, Seurat, Gauguin, and Van Gogh; though they may have shown little interest in Monet's experiments, they owe a debt to Impressionism.

CÉZANNE. Cézanne's specifically Impressionist period was brief. In Pontoise and later in Auvers, Pissarro had initiated him into the interrelation of light and color, and his years of working with Pissarro were to become decisive for his artistic development. It was there that he discarded the dark, heavy pigments of his earlier works in favor of small, rapid brush strokes better suited to the reproduction of the wealth of nuances in nature. In his desire to gain a better understanding of Pissarro's technique, he even made exact copies of Pissarro's Louveciennes landscapes. Yet, though Cézanne's major works were no longer the product of pure Impressionism, its influence on him was sufficiently great to make him a legitimate subject in any discussion of this movement. Unlike the Impressionists, who, working rapidly, attempted to capture a given moment in nature, Cézanne achieved a symphony of color through patient, industrious application. In his work, classical composition, neglected since Monet, again came to the fore. Cézanne's world is dense, solid, stable, and—above all—pictorial. The apples he painted have none of the delicacy and sensuality of Dutch still lifes: they are pure painting. It is this sort of realism which transforms the object almost to the point of nonrecognition which "ordinary common sense" rejects in Cézanne's work and, beyond that, in all modern art.

Cézanne was too consistent, too much of a classicist, not to see the unimportance of the "little sensation," of the stubborn and pointless pursuit of optical effects. It was these qualities which helped him to evolve his own type of Impressionism—"something

SISLEY. BANKS OF THE SEINE IN AUTUMN. STÄDELSCHES KUNSTINSTITUT, FRANKFURT.

Sisley, an Impressionist par excellence, *remained faithful to the "small sensation" for the whole of his life. There was no real development in his work, as there was in that of Monet ; he remained faithful to his vision of the years 1872-1875, but his style became mannered. "Despite his finical, glittering, flickering touch," wrote J.-E. Blanche, "his work was somewhat arid, and he only succeeded in capturing the vibrations of the atmosphere with an erratic pseudo-Pointillism, the monotonous laborious work in the style of a Raffaelli." There is always the same subtlety of tone, the same atmospheric delicacy, but the excessive chromatic finesse so destroys the solidity of the composition that it dissolves. Later, the painter realized what had happened and became aware of the need to build up a canvas with a foreground of verticals and a large diagonal. But the effect was too contrived and became decorative.*

lasting, like the art in museums"— to "recreate Poussin from nature." His analysis of Impressionism was useful to him in arriving at a geometric, abstract conception analogous to that of

CÉZANNE. HARLEQUIN. C. 1888. ART INSTITUTE, CHICAGO.

CÉZANNE. BATHERS. 1879-1882. BOYMANS MUSEUM, ROTTERDAM.

the great masters of the past, but one which had a pictorial quality
not found in the canvases of the old masters.   In his attempt to
"see" his subject—he almost can be said to have identified himself
with it—he remained faithful to Pissarro's vision.   "One is neither
too careful, nor too conscientious, nor too much enthralled by
nature," he once said, "but, more or less, one is the master of one's
models and, above all, of one's means of expression."   And as a
matter of fact, the more he strove to discipline his brush, to escape
"the infernal facility of the brush," the greater became the warmth
of his technique.   He waged a fierce, exhausting struggle for style
and for truth.

"*Little by little, Cézanne discovered that behind the monochrome façade of objects looked at intellectually—white tablecloth, gray stone, black cloth, red apple, green salad—that is to say, as one learns to see them in context of their daily use, there are hidden iridescences or, to use his own term, 'modulations,' which transform the appearance of these objects to the point of rendering them unrecognizable. . . . This misunderstanding increased when Cézanne noticed that the objects changed not only in color but in form. . . that, despite their material differences, it was permissible for the cloth on the table, the fruit-dish, and the bottle to assume a similar silken effect which reduced them, so to speak, to a common denominator; but that a table, when its line was broken by the back of a chair*

CÉZANNE. ONIONS AND BOTTLE. 1895-1900.
LOUVRE, PARIS.

CÉZANNE. STILL LIFE WITH A CHEST OF DRAWERS. 1883-1887.
BAYERISCHE STAATSGEMÄLDESAMMLUNGEN, MUNICH.

*or a spread cloth, should be split into two divergent parts which
according to the most elementary laws of carpentry could not be
joined ; that the edges of the fruit-dish should appear straight at the
front and exaggeratedly curved elsewhere ; that the bottle itself,
suffering the same fate, should have one of its bulging sides flattened
and the curve of the other accentuated ; that, furthermore, the bottle
'should lean over as if about to fall'—all these constituted intolerable liberties which mocked the orthodox. But the orthodox in art
are not always those who feel the most strongly. For Cézanne,
nothing in painting mattered except sensation."* André Lhote.

141

Primarily, Cézanne was concerned with emotional response to color and, through the mastery of this response, with geometric representation of nature, a representation enlivened with contrasts of vibrant reds and yellows and blue shadows. The Impressionists were familiar with emotional reactions to color, they knew the value of blue and orange harmonies (with blue representing pure shadow and orange absolute light); but Cézanne had an additional gift, something they lacked—and Lionello Venturi defined this as "the immediate moment of structure and of the geometric ideal in which Cézanne's intellectual power found the essential element of his style."

For Cézanne, painting never meant the slavish copying of an object; he wanted to encompass what he himself called "a harmony of numerous facets," and his attempt to achieve this goal is probably the real reason for the "grotesque distortion" of his *Bathers*—and not, as has been charged, either the moral scruples of Mme. Cézanne or the painter's modesty which supposedly prevented him from doing a nude from life. Such explanations fail to take into account the essentials governing the structure of a picture, those factors without which no painting could ever be the equivalent, the pictorial circumscription, of reality. If Cézanne painted from memory, he did so because the subject had ceased to be of primary importance to him, because he wished to free himself of the fetters the subject imposes on the artist. The monumental figure of the *Bather* in the Museum of Modern Art collection testifies to Cézanne's ability to preserve the innate human dignity of the individual and thus achieve a universality, even when working from a photograph of a rather ridiculous-looking model. Cézanne believed that the human figure represented the "culmination of art," and his portraits, so carefully and scrupulously executed, have an aura of lucidity and imposing gravity, an almost masklike quality. Cézanne gave the world a new concept of humanity; he opened new vistas; he traveled new roads which others after him followed.

GAUGUIN. Books on the history of art usually group Gauguin, as well as Cézanne and Van Gogh, with the Impressionists. Indeed, Paul Gauguin did begin within the framework of Impressionism when, as a respectable Paris banker, he started painting under Pissarro's direction. That he had long been interested in the movement is demonstrated by the fact that he had already built up a private collection of Manets, Jongkinds, Cézannes, Renoirs, Monets, Pissarros, and Sisleys. In 1879, he began exhibiting with the Impressionists, but he was, in fact, an heir to their tradition, not a member. He said that the Impressionists "studied color for its decorative effect only; they remained fettered to the idea of likenesses and, as a result, they lacked freedom. . . . They had an image, a harmonious image, but it is an aimless one. . . . They

GAUGUIN. HEADS OF TAHITIAN WOMEN.

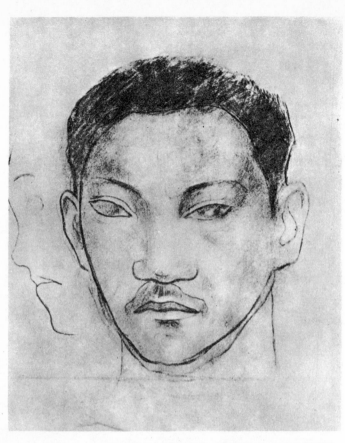

GAUGUIN. TAHITIAN. PRIVATE COLLECTION.

explored visual effects rather than the mysterious core of ideas, and thus they fell into scientific theorization."

By 1885, Impressionism was in a state of flux; it had become nothing more than a name, embracing as many trends as there were artists who tried to claim it as their own. Gauguin broke the bonds of the superrefined naturalism into which Impressionism had fallen. In his search for a individual style, he initially tried to emulate Cézanne and then Seurat, until finally he found the elements

"*Savage !   This word came inevitably to my mind when I regarded these black creatures with their cannibal teeth.   Already, however, I had caught a glimpse of their real grace. . . .   I was for them something to be observed, the unknown, the one who knew neither the language nor even the simplest and most natural actions of life.   As they were for me, so I was for them the 'savage.'   And perhaps it was I who was wrong.*"   Gauguin.

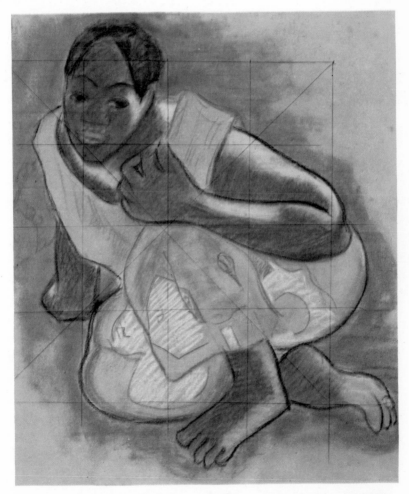

GAUGUIN. TAHITIAN CROUCHING. C. 1892. ART INSTITUTE, CHICAGO.

of his method in the work of Émile Bernard—a tonal scale restricted to six primary, "not too natural" colors, bounded by dark outlines and a flattened perspective—elements reminiscent of ancient Egyptian art, Roman frescoes, Japanese woodcuts, and possibly the naïve primitivism of Kate Greenaway illustrations.

Baudelaire once spoke of "recreating a universe governed by intellect with the help of factors selected according to a definite order and hierarchy," and this was Gauguin's guiding ambition also. Creativity was to follow "a subjective logic"; it was to transpose reality through the arbitrary use of color and form. Gauguin, attempting in *Noa-Noa* to create a work akin to Rimbaud's *Bateau Ivre*, became his own prisoner, held captive in the sharply defined, fragile world of intellectualism. He created an unmistakable, individual style. This breaking away from painting, this new approach which no longer had any real contact with the world, inevitably had to end in disillusionment; hence his colors which so shocked his contemporaries, hence the distortions predicated on the rhythm and color of his paintings. Gauguin said that he wanted the right to experiment as he saw fit, and that his daring had paved the way for the most subjective abstractions. Gauguin may have thought of himself as a creator of abstract compositions, but in reality he created decorative canvases. Paintings which no longer attempted to suggest tridimensionalism—a deceptive and intolerable convention, he felt—once again became flat surfaces. Henceforth, painting was to be flat and even, without nuances of tone, with homogeneous, harmonic colors outlined by clearly defined strokes. Thus, line and color would achieve an equilibrium and approach the ideal of static serenity suitable for murals, the antithesis of the Impressionist ideal. Gauguin—headstrong, believing in the supremacy of instinct—went to the far corners of the earth in search of that which he had initially rejected. His obsession with color, which he pushed to

GAUGUIN. ÈVE. WOODCUT. BIBLIOTHÈQUE NATIONALE, PARIS.

the furthest possible extreme, to the point of complete dissimilarity, was summed up by him as follows: "How do you see this shadow? Rather on the blue side? Then don't be afraid to paint it as blue

GAUGUIN. TAHITIANS ON THE BEACH. 1891-1892.
ROBERT LEHMAN COLLECTION, NEW YORK.

as possible." This was the essence of the triumphant vision of Impressionism, yet Gauguin did not see himself as an Impressionist.

V AN G OGH . The world of form is a finite and limited one of which we have only a vague conscious awareness, and one which painting attempts to reproduce. Impressionist art, though indisputably sensuous, remains an art of renunciation, not concerning itself with probing the depths of emotions, but merely wishing to transmit the image perceived by the senses. Hence, Van Gogh cannot be classed among the Impressionists; in his art, he sought to define the spiritual link between man and the universe. He had none of the modernity of Impressionism. Van Gogh was the painter of the universal. There is no other artist whose work is imbued with the same sense of the tragic as is his, and it is this sense of the tragic which formed the basis of his relationship to his art. He was obsessed by something which transcended painting and which shaped his extraordinary life. History has, of course, known numerous great creative artists who have experienced profound tragedy, and their tortured cries still echo through all the museums of the world. But the shattering reality of Van Gogh's image of man's relentless universal conflict—culminating in the artist's own madness—seemed like a symbol of his fate to his contemporaries. It would be a misinterpretation of his work, though, to see it only as a symbol. Such a view obliterates the deep roots and the supreme achievement of his creativity, leaving only the unique, extraordinary aspect of his life.

"I must," he said, "continue along the road I am going, because if I did nothing, if I ceased in my search, I would be lost. Then woe to me." Where did Van Gogh stand in July, 1880, when at twenty-seven years of age he realized that painting was his vocation ? What did he do, whom did he study, what did he search

for ? His travels had taken him away from and back to his homeland—Holland, land of rich autumnal harvests, of desolate, storm-
racked winters, a land of misty gray horizons bordering on a gray
ocean. Van Gogh became preoccupied with the never-ending
dialogue between shadow and light, the same obsession with the
land which had dominated Dutch painting since Rembrandt. His
feeling for the land explains Van Gogh's admiration for Millet
and the Barbizon school. He identified himself with the silent
poverty depicted in the soul-searching canvases of Courbet and
Cézanne. Ever since his youth, he had known that to him "nature,
clods of earth, yellow corn, peasants were not only symbols of
work, but also sources of consolation and strength." This same
feeling of warm compassion, this incurable melancholy never was
to leave him—either in the meadows of his homeland or in the

VAN GOGH, SHEAVES OF CORN, 1888.
COLLECTION DR. HANS R. HAHNLOSER, WINTERTHUR.

VAN GOGH. THE ANGLOIS BRIDGE. 1888.
G. GARD DE SYLVA COLLECTION, LOS ANGELES.

sooty mining settlements of the Borinage. He was one with these oppressed, patient people, filled with century-old memories of misery and with an elemental longing for the earth. Van Gogh thought that he had been called by God; he had wanted to give himself to this world of misery, and the world had refused to accept him. There was nothing else left for him but to withdraw into himself, "to keep his inner flame burning, to wait for the hour which had to come." He had attended "the free course at the great university of misery, had cared for things," and his heart was rent by love and pity. He had loved "with great and exalted inner sympathy, with purpose and intelligence," and he always wanted "to seek a greater and better understanding," because it was essential to find—and paint—that truth within one's own heart

"What made Seurat a complete painter was that, though uniquely capable of translating the drama of light and shade by the rudimentary means of chiaroscuro, he was not content with this success and, in the wake of the Impressionists, consecrated all his talent to replacing the specific elements of drawing—black, white, and gray— by their equivalents in the solar spectrum—warm colors for light tones, cold colors for the dark ones, and an intermingling of the two for neutral colors or intermediate tints. Admittedly, this can be found in the work of all the Impressionists and is superbly apparent in that of Cézanne ; but Seurat was the only one who simultaneously concerned himself with values and color, depending on whether he was drawing or painting. . ." André Lhote.

SEURAT. HONFLEUR, BOUT DE LA JETÉE. 1886.
RIJKSMUSEUM KRÖLLER-MÜLLER, OTTERLO.

PISSARRO. L'ILE LACROIX, ROUEN. FOG EFFECT. 1888.
JOHN G. JOHNSON COLLECTION, MUSEUM OF ART, PHILADELPHIA.

Pissarro, who met Seurat through Signac, was won over by Seurat's seriousness and his scientific method. Forsaking his friends, he became the defender of Neo-Impressionism. He continued in this role until he realized the folly of the orthodox adherence to a system which does not express the individual temperament of the artist. Nevertheless, this short association of Pissarro with the younger generation inspired some very fine works of exceptional perception, like this view of the river on a misty morning.

which is the key to the secret and the salvation of man.   He sought salvation—for himself, for his brothers, for his companions—in his long vigils with the sick, by sharing his bread with the poor, by going naked to clothe the nakedness of others.   But compassion did not spell deliverance; he was aware that something was false and missing in his life.   He turned to painting with the same passionate love with which he had turned to God earlier.   Painting became his means for deliverance from the sense of imprisonment that engulfed him.   And thus was born that gigantic impulse which was to lead him through the depths of darkness to the most extreme delirium of color.

Working by himself in The Hague, Van Gogh evolved his own technique.   There, too, in 1883, he took Christine, a poor, wretched prostitute, to live with him.   Christine became a symbol of human misery to him, but she brought nothing but scandal and misunderstanding into his life.   Everything he did seemed to go wrong.   He who wanted nothing more than peace became involved in exhausting daily domestic scenes.   "Life has taken on the colors of dirty water, it resembles a heap of ashes."   Throughout these dark days, however, he was possessed of one certainty: "Within a few years I must complete a definite task."

In 1885, he left for Antwerp, and there he accidentally came across some Japanese woodcuts which made a deep impression on him.   They seemed like symbols of the East, of the sun.   In 1886, he left for Paris, where he met the Impressionists whom his faithful brother Theo, an employee of the art dealer Goupil, had told him about.   Here, for the first time, Van Gogh lived among artists, among men who were concerned with nothing but painting.   Although his letters to Theo in earlier years reveal that he had already been much concerned with the problem of color, these encounters with painters brought him new insights into the uses of color.   Impressionism to him seemed to offer the possibility of

metarmophosis.   Under its influence he was able to rid himself of
the darkness within him, of his missionary zeal, of loneliness.   He
set out to conquer space and depth.   In the unthought-of possibilities of color, he discovered a means of salvation.   He discovered
himself, his roots, and his inner necessity.   He went from discovery
to discovery: green, blue, red, and green—juxtaposed, scattered
about— can change the relationship between the universe and the
artist.

   It took him less than two years to conquer this world of the
"small sensations" of Impressionism.   His hunger for new colors
drove him onward—to the south of France, in search of the secret
of the sun which he had glimpsed in the paintings of Monticelli

SIGNAC. WOMAN DOING HER HAIR. 1892. GINETTE SIGNAC COLLECTION, PARIS.

"*In front of a blank canvas, the first preoccupation of a painter should be to decide what curves and what arabesques are to cut across the surface, what colors and what tones are to cover it. . . . The Neo-Impressionist, following the advice of Delacroix, will not embark on a canvas without having first determined the main pattern. . . . He will attune the composition to his conception, in other words, he will adapt the lines (directions and angles), the chiaroscuro (tones), and the colors (tints) to what he intends shall be the prevailing character. The dominant lines are: horizontal*

SEURAT. LA POUDREUSE (MADELEINE KNOBLOCH). 1889-1890.
COURTAULD INSTITUTE, LONDON.

*lines for calmness ; ascending lines for joy ; descending lines for
sadness. All intermediate lines are used to represent all the other
sensations in their infinite variety. A polychromatic interplay, no
less expressive or varied, is added to the linear one: warm colors
and light tones correspond to ascending lines ; with descending lines,
cold colors and dark tones predominate, a more or less perfect balance
between pale and intense tones adds to the calm of horizontal lines."*
Signac.

and in the Japanese woodcuts. At Arles, he was greeted by snow and silvery olive trees, by yellow rocks and green cypresses, by lemon trees and the soil of the vineyards. But however beautiful was this reality, it failed to satisfy his inner vision of a metamorphosis. In his landscapes, portraits, and interiors, his compulsion forced him to upset the outer order and substitute for it the magical and miraculous in all their confusion. He was obsessed by his work, painting day and night. He bathed himself in sun and light, in a symphony of orange and blue, in the richness of a sleeping world. He explored the red and black of night in the depth of the human eye, in phosphorescent skies shrouding cornfields and houses. Like the development of a musical theme by two instruments, his paintings have a contrapuntal quality, with salvation and damnation as their two themes. At times, Van Gogh seemed to realize that the conflict was irreconcilable, and then the period of darkness enveloped him. After the visit of Gauguin, whom he had called to Arles in the hope that they could work together; after the quarrel which was to separate them forever, after his self-mutilation—he voluntarily entered the asylum at Saint-Rémy. Obsessed by the thought of madness, he became less concerned with color than with movement. He began painting in a sort of delirious rhythm, with great writhing curves swirling above olive trees and cypresses. Occasionally, above the wild colors of night, his portraits and flowers showed a note of calm, a note of hopelessness. He was haunted by memories of his homeland, and in his whitewashed cottages and muddy paths, his colors took on a softness. Anxiety, melancholia, and nostalgia plagued him relentlessly. He felt guilt-ridden, overwhelmed by solitude. He tortured himself with feelings of failure, with guilt for letting his brother support him; he suffered under the feeling that his very existence depended on the good will and help of others.

In the spring of 1890, he left the south of France to live with

Dr. Gachet at Auvers-sur-Oise. In the short period of two months, he painted innumerable canvases, both portraits and landscapes. Some were happy and relaxed compositions in green and pink, others terrible, dark, depressed paintings full of the sense of impending doom—pictures full of the longing for peace, for the lulling safety of the wind-combed soil. On July 27, he went out to hunt crows, and there, in the fields, he shot himself. He died two days later, on a brilliant summer morning.

Vincent Van Gogh had found his destiny and died in wild rebellion against misery and insanity. He left the world more than merely the heritage of a painter whose inner vision transformed man's picture of the world. He lost his life and his sanity in search of the true content of life.

TOULOUSE-LAUTREC. Henri de Toulouse-Lautrec, like Degas, was of aristocratic descent, and, as did Degas, he liked to record "moments of interest" in the lives of women. Women, lovers, bars, ballrooms, brothels, the world of high society—all these were subjected to Toulouse-Lautrec's scrutiny; all ranges of human experience fascinated him. He was much more than a mere chronicler of his era. He painted his subjects—Grille-d'Égout, La Goulue, Yvette Guilbert, Tristan Bernard, Henry Nocq, Maxime Dethomas—with a mixture of amusement and sadness, with humor and affection. Society at its lowest ebb was his favorite setting and his inspiration. He penetrated the protective masks of the poor, miserable people he painted, never condemning, never judging; if he was cruel, his cruelty was only his own particular brand of irony. The land of sun where Gauguin drowned himself in alcohol and the terrible hell through which the crippled Lautrec dragged himself represented something quite similar for each: in both, two artists searched for an unattainable happiness and discovered the core of suffering in all human existence. The whole *fin de siècle*

After the experimental Haystacks *and* Poplars *series, Monet painted nearly forty* Rouen Cathedrals *between 1893 and 1895. These works—always the same façade with no earth or sky—record*

MONET. ROUEN CATHEDRAL IN FULL SUNLIGHT. 1894.
LOUVRE, PARIS.

MONET. ROUEN CATHEDRAL IN SUNLIGHT. 1894. LOUVRE, PARIS.

the variations of light during the course of a single day. But the struggle between the artist who wishes to capture the moment and the light which continually changes the motif is an unequal one.

misery can be found in this senseless desire to lose or find oneself in the company of beautiful Tahitian girls or of Boulevard de Clichy prostitutes plying their trade.

To Lautrec, the elegance of Degas—haughty and heartless— seemed sterile. Lautrec, warm and compassionate, admired Degas, but he did not imitate him. However, these two men shared one consuming passion. They both loved horses, thorough-breds. What mattered to them in art was the mysterious appeal of the line, the definition of the object. They did not want to be duped about anything, and especially about their art. The line was the uncompromising mark of analysis, of comprehension, of discipline. This was also the lesson taught by the Japanese. But Lautrec expressed that which they had only hinted at, and at the

TOULOUSE-LAUTREC. THE DRINKER. 1889. MUSÉE D'ALBI.

TOULOUSE-LAUTREC. THE CABARET SINGER ARISTIDE BRUANT.

same time he gave his work a substance and power which the Japanese lacked. His posters were an almost inevitable result of his development. The boldness of composition, the sureness and power of line, the use of color, and the color contrasts which lithography made possible—these were Lautrec's contribution to poster art. He was captivated by this new art form—alive yet ephemeral—which demanded an impudent style and brevity of expression. Lautrec's posters created such a stir when they first appeared in 1896 that a "league for the protection of public morality" had large pictures of scenes from the life of Sainte Geneviève by Puvis de Chavannes pasted over them. This act sealed Lautrec's success. "The museum has moved to the streets, and this is only the beginning," said Maurice Maindron. Thanks to posters, there no longer was a gap between living art and the public, save in the minds of those who thought that only dead artists were good artists.

Lautrec's studies and variations of the self-same theme did not attempt to capture momentary effects, they were not meant as the notations of a reporter. They were his unceasing constructive attempts to achieve the perfect synthesis, and in this manner he arrived at the essential content of his art. That which easily could have become a pattern in fact became the ideal type, the idea. The Moulin-Rouge and the rest of Paris at night which he painted so often would easily have lent themselves to a scandalized or romanticized interpretation. But Lautrec rejected such easy solutions, alien to his concept of art. In his pictures, La Goulue, despite her obvious faults, became the incarnation of the dance. His themes, even more than his interpretation of them, were a reflection of the French and Munich schools at the turn of the century; seen from such a perspective, Lautrec's art could be relegated to the "trend" of his era were it not for his highly individual graphic style, particularly in his posters. Lautrec's people, so Gustave Moreau told his pupils, were painted "in absinthe."

TOULOUSE-LAUTREC. YVETTE GUILBERT. 1891-189
PUSHKIN MUSEUM, MOSCOW.

10

THE FINAL TRIUMPH,
PUBLIC ACCEPTANCE

TODAY, when exhibitions of Impressionist art attract huge crowds, it is hard to believe that for thirty years the Impressionists were treated as social outcasts and their work subjected to the scathing attacks of art critics. But this was actually so until the last few years of the nineteenth century. The Impressionists had to flee Paris, they were unwanted, almost all of them had to lead a hand-to-mouth existence. Rarely before had the battle of creative artists against obscurantism and prejudice demanded such a degree of self-denial, tenacity, and faith, and without the friendship and enthusiasm of a handful of collectors and art dealers they probably would not have been able to survive those years of ostracism and deprivation. It was the art dealers who ultimately helped to open the eyes of the public and to gain acceptance for the Impressionists. It is not at all surprising that museum curators, being as conformist as the rest of painting officialdom, were not exactly eager to acquire Impressionist art. Impartial artistic evaluation was not the motivating factor in museum acquisitions; curators dodged decisions which could compromise their positions. Léonce Benedite, Curator of the Musée du Luxembourg, said: "The state has as little business to lay down official aesthetic laws as it has to lay down official religious or moral laws; museums should confine themselves to presenting the facts, the works of art, in a logical

VAN GOGH. SUNSET NEAR SAINT-RÉMY. 1889-1890. NEUE STAATSGALERIE, MUNICH.

chronology; the public must have the right to draw its own conclusions." But these fine words were merely a cloak for the shoddy politics of the museums, which were busily acquiring the platitudinous works of pseudo-Impressionists—of Bastien-Lepage, Besnard, Henri-Martin, and all the others who knew how to please the tastes of the "right people." Instead of the works of Manet and Seurat and Degas, the museums acquired paintings by Stevens and Gaston La Touche and J.-E. Blanche and Ernest Laurent and

In 1896, an eye inflammation prevented Pissarro from continuing his open-air painting, and he was forced to move to the city. But he did not give up painting altogether and during the next two years, depending on where he was living, he created a number of views of Rouen and Paris. Attracted by the vision of vast horizons, he worked from his window in the Hôtel de Russie on the corner of the Rue Drouet and the Grands Boulevards, in the Hôtel du Louvre in the Rue de Rivoli, in his apartment in the Boulevard Henri IV, and finally at 28 Place Dauphine. These plunging views with their light coloring are reminiscent of Pointillism and are animated by an intense love of life which the old artist contemplated with almost ingenuous feelings of wonder.

C. Pissarro. 98

many more like them. All these competent practitioners of their trade—the darlings of the Luxembourg— were able to fool the critics, and the honest, conscientious art historians, fearful of making a mistake, never departed from the old, established criteria of composition and execution. In all fairness, it must be admitted that men like Bonnat, Ribot, and Carolus Duran were painters, but they were not the geniuses they believed themselves to be. They possessed nothing more than pleasant talents.

Who today would doubt the business acumen of a dealer who buys Impressionists? But when Durand-Ruel bought Pissarros, Monets, Renoirs, Manets, and Sisleys, when he gave these artists all the financial and moral support he could, his actions were certainly not viewed as constituting a major business coup. In fact, he failed to find a single buyer for the canvases. But he never gave up, even when he found himself deeply in debt, even when those on whom he had pinned all his hopes deserted him. It took twenty years for his persistence to be rewarded. Bad paintings pay off more quickly and are much better business.

There was also old Père Tanguy, the dealer in artists' materials, who once said: "Whoever lives on more than fifty centimes a day is a scoundrel." The financial help that people of such principles were able to give was necessarily limited, but Père Tanguy did what he could, and he was frequently the last hope of the artists. In selling paintings at a fixed price, he did not expect to make a fortune: 100 francs for a large Cézanne, 40 francs for a small one. After his death in 1894, his widow was forced to sell the canvases which Monet, Cézanne, Seurat, and Van Gogh had given her husband as collateral, and she considered herself fortunate to receive 14,621 francs for the lot of them. For many years, Père Tanguy's shop was the museum of Impressionism. According to Émile Bernard, "One went there as if to a museum. Members of the

RENOIR. GABRIELLE WITH JEAN RENOIR. 1895.
PRIVATE COLLECTION.

Institute, influential, up-to-date critics sought out his unpretentious little shop, which became the talk of Paris and of the studios."

The case of Ambroise Vollard was more complex. We may never know for sure whether his support of Impressionist art was motivated by conviction or if he was guided by a gambler's instinct. It took courage for him—the little clerk who peddled the drawings with which Félicien Rops, Bonnard, and Lautrec settled their café bills—to try to make money with the works of those artists who had been rejected by the Salon, particularly with those of Cézanne, whom even Durand-Ruel ignored. At that time, it was not enough to be the subject of a scandal in order to gain a reputation for genius, and the art business was much more precarious than it is today. The sort of bold vision that was responsible for Vollard's sponsorship of the first all-Cézanne exhibition in 1895 deserved the financial rewards he reaped later when he numbered his clients the American collector Havemeyer and King Milan of Serbia.

By no stretch of the imagination did the early friends and collectors of the Impressionists consider themselves heroes. They loved among painting, and as far as they were concerned, that was all that mattered. They never remotely concerned themselves with the possibility of future profits. As a matter of fact, they sometimes went without in order to help their painter-friends. Among these early friends was the customs inspector Chocquet, whose admiration for Delacroix brought him almost automatically to Manet, Monet, Renoir, and Cézanne. He first encountered Impressionist art at Durand-Ruel's auction of 1875, and he was won over immediately. He became a patron of the group; he bought their paintings, lent them money, and defended them passionately. When he divested himself of his collection in 1899, it included thirty-two Cézannes, eleven Monets, eleven Renoirs, five Manets, one Pissarro, and one Sisley. Other early supporters included the publisher Charpentier, Théodore Duret, the actor Faure—and, above all, Gustave Caillebotte, an amateur painter and a most devoted friend. A man of means, Caillebotte bought works whose sales potential seemed most unpromising. "Nobody wants them? In that case I will buy them." His collection grew rapidly, and because he did not want it broken up, he decided to will it to the state. The presen-

RENOIR. IN THE MEADOW. C. 1895.
SAM A. LEWISOHN BEQUEST, METROPOLITAN MUSEUM OF ART, NEW YORK.

tation in 1897 caused a furor.   The Institute fumed; its members threatened to resign; Roujon, the head of the École des Beaux-Arts, and Benedite, the Curator of the Musée du Luxembourg, did not want the state to accept the gift, and it required all the power of persuasion of Renoir, who was executor of Caillebotte's estate, to arrive at a compromise solution.   The conditions of the will had to be changed and the collection reduced by twenty-seven paintings in order to have it accepted by the museum.   And it took a public petition to force the Louvre to accept Manet's *Olympia*.   In later years, the government collection was enlarged with donations by Moreau-Nélaton in 1906 and by Isaac de Camondo in 1911.   The fight for acceptance was definitely won when Monet left his *Water Lilies* to the state in 1922.

Outside France, Impressionism also had a checkered career.   In the United States, the fight on behalf of this new art form was not so difficult, since there was no old, established national tradition to overcome.   On the contrary, Durand-Ruel as well as artists like Mary Cassatt, William M. Chase, and Maurice Prendergast were able to interest a number of prominent collectors in the acquisition of Impressionists.   In England, recognition did not come so quickly, and it was largely due to the efforts of Courtauld that Impressionism came to be accepted after the end of World War I. Courbet, who had spent some time both in Munich and Frankfurt, was indirectly responsible for introducing Impressionist art to Germany.   There a battle had to be fought against the hundred-year-old supremacy of the Düsseldorf school.   The Munich International Exhibition of 1869 was the occasion for the first public show-ing of new, naturalistic art.   On this occasion, the German painter Leibl and Courbet scored the greatest successes.   The Munich Exhibition also showed canvases by Chintreuil, Daubigny, Harpi-gnies, Millet, Corot, and Manet.   Although these artists (with the exception of Manet) were not exactly Impressionists, they did however make the first breach in the bastions of the prevailing sentimental romanticism.   In 1891, works of French Impressionists were shown alongside those of German painters at the Munich Exhibition.   And it was Hugo von Tschudi, the director of the Berlin National Gallery, who, with the help of Max Liebermann, brought Manet, Cézanne, Gauguin, and Van Gogh into German museums in 1896, an act which cost him his position.   This happened at the same time that efforts were being made to gain entrance into the Louvre for the Caillebotte Collection.   It is interesting to note that all the Manets and Monets to be found in the museums of Bremen, Mannheim, and Munich were initially chosen for their naturalistic qualities.   This initiative of the collectors, of the museums, and particularly of the art dealer Paul Cassirer, whose brother Bruno published *Kunst und Künstler* (the Impressionist art forum), had a decisive influence on the development of the *Jugendstil,* the German *art nouveau.*

Thanks to Diaghilev and the Moscow art dealer Shchukin, French Impressionist art was already to be found in great Russian collections before the end of the nineteenth century.   But the presence of revolutionary paintings in collections amassed by the aristocracy had little effect on Russian art and artists.   The snobbish collectors had no contact with the creative youth of their country.   It was the art review *Solotoe Runo* ("The Golden Fleece") which spread knowledge about the Impressionists and which sponsored an exhibit in 1909 of the works of Cézanne, Gauguin, Van Gogh, and Lautrec, as well as of Matisse, Rouault, and Bracque.   This new art, with its radical departure from all academic tradition, was to make a startling impression on young painters like Chagall, Malevitch, Kandinsky, and Larionov, who went to Germany—to Berlin and Munich—in search of this new liberating French art.   However, Impressionism was too specifically French

PISSARRO. RUE DE L'ÉPICERIE AT ROUEN. 1898.

to have a lasting effect on foreign artists. But considered as a
moral attitude rather than a technique, it proved to be of decisive
importance to all of European art.

Although Belgian literary development of this period paralleled

PISSARRO. RUE DE L'ÉPICERIE AT ROUEN, GRAY MORNING. 1898.
PRIVATE COLLECTION, PARIS.

that of neighboring France, Belgian art remained autonomous. Faithful to the Flemish tradition of naturalism, Belgian painting did not succumb to Impressionism. The Belgians were too earthy to adopt a technique which seemed to them like an intellectual game. The brief Impressionist period of Jakob Smits, Ensor, and Evenopoel was primarily a reaction against the realism of Braekelaer, yet it helped to pave the way for the Fauvism of Wouters and the Expressionism of Permeke and Smet.

In other European countries, the world of art was dominated by official academism or by a jealously guarded obsolete naturalism, supposedly an expression of unique national characteristics. True, there was a movement in Italy in 1858 which resembled French Impressionism, the "Macchiaioli" movement—a form of Tachism which flourished in Florence long before this word was known— but it had no sequel. The French influence was also discernible in the late works of Domenico Morelli, and in the canvases of Segantini, the Nittis, and Boldoni. But they were mere followers of a style, insufficiently individualistic to be considered true creators.

In Spain—Goya's Spain, which exerted such a strong influence on Manet—Sorolla and Rusiñol were to discover the magic qualities of light toward the end of the nineteenth century. But it was the young Pablo Ruiz Picasso who, with the help of Ramon Casas and his friends from Barcelona, learned the lesson that Impressionism had to teach. His first Paris canvas—*Moulin de la Galette,* painted in 1900—and his early canvases of dance halls, cafés, concerts, and circuses displayed a brilliance and intensity reminiscent of Toulouse-Lautrec. They formed the beginning of the most disturbing and, at the same time, the most tremendous adventure in art of modern times.

NEO-IMPRESSIONISM
AND SYMBOLISM

IMPRESSIONISM—purely pictorial in conception—exerted no influence on the literature of its period. Writers believed in the power of the word. They were confused by that element in painting which could not be put into words. The same critics who defended Manet and Monet in the name of realism and naturalism recoiled once they realized that this new art was less concerned with ideas than with emotions. And the objectivity which Pissarro, Renoir, and Cézanne sought for (but which, in fact, was only a seeming objectivity) was allied with a scientific tendency which repelled the next generation of writers. Art, as far as they were concerned, could not be imitative; its function was the discovery of the hidden meaning of things. They believed in the secret relationship between the visible and the invisible, the same relationship that exists between sound and smell and color. Nature was a veil spread over the hidden truth of creation, and the revelation of this truth demanded an inner vision, a liberation from the formalism of the object, the overcoming and destruction of the illusion of objectivity. "I should like to see red meadows, golden-yellow rivers, and trees painted blue. Nature has no imagination." These words of Baudelaire foreshadowed Gauguin's dream and his attempt to escape from reality. " In the face of nature, it is our imagination which paints the picture." The dream conflicted

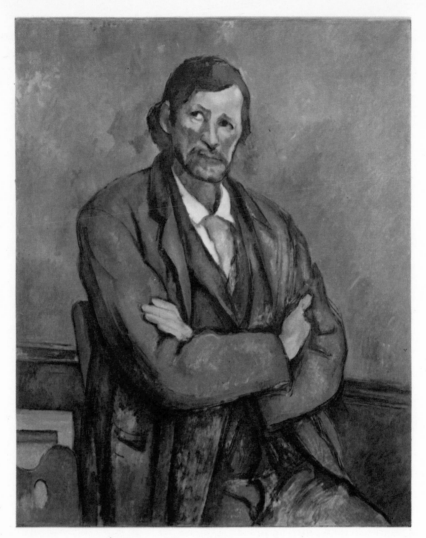

CÉZANNE. THE CLOCKMAKER. 1895-1900.
SOLOMON R. GUGGENHEIM MUSEUM, NEW YORK.

After 1895, Cézanne's portraits lost their serene objectivity and the old master returned to the baroque vein of his earliest works. More and more, he unconsciously substituted his own features for those of his model as if, faced with a model, it was really himself whom he sought to decipher.

with reality, and in their search for new sources of inspirations the artists turned toward mythology, Rosicrucianism, the occult, the music of Wagner, the Pre-Raphaelites, and new ideologies like socialism and anarchism. It was inevitable that painting suffered, even though the best exponents of this trend—Eugène Carrière, James Ensor, and Odilon Redon—were able to find new harmonies of unexpected richness of line and design amidst this confusion; for any attempt to borrow analogies from other fields was bound to reduce it to mere illustration and decoration, however attractive. Redon attempted to explore the subconscious, and with the help of chiaroscuro he succeeded in depicting the twilight stages of the soul. The Symbolists, denigrating the Impressionist method which they mistakenly identified with Claude Bernard and the positivism of Comte, believed themselves heir to the lyrical tradition of Delacroix and reaffirmed the supremacy of the spirit. To Gauguin, Impressionism was nothing but "a sensitive enumeration of the elements of the world and an inventory of its physical charms," a superficial art, "all coquetry, wholly material. "

After seeing Gauguin's *Vision After the Sermon,* painted in 1888 at Pont-Aven, the critic Albert Aurier defined the principles of Symbolism in the *Mercure de France* of March, 1891, in these words: "First, the work of art will be *conceptual,* since its one ideal will be the expression of an idea; second, *symbolic,* because it will express the idea through form; third, *synthetic,* because these forms and symbols will be presented in a generally comprehensible manner; fifth (as a logical result), *decorative,* because basically, decorative painting is nothing but a simultaneously subjective, synthetic, symbolic, and conceptual expression of art."

In point of fact, however, the idea behind symbolic painting is rather vapid. Puvis de Chavannes, who wished to ignore the achievements of a Monet, was inspired by this sort of anemic idealism, a mixture of misinterpreted antiquity and equally misconstrued medievalism. Gauguin, on the other hand, attracted to and appreciative of primitive art, was merely anti-intellectual. His attitude toward Puvis de Chavannes, whom he admired, was summed up in the following words: "True, he expresses his ideas, but he doesn't paint them. He is a Greek, whereas I am a savage." Gauguin, despite his critical attitude toward Impressionism, was careful not to dismiss every one of its accomplishments; he took with him to Tahiti the Impressionist concern with reproducing pure sensation.

J. Alvard wrote that the Impressionists awakened man to life, that their being was suffused by nature, but that this passive submission to nature necessarily resulted in a withdrawal into oneself. This and similar analyses and meditations on the nature of Impressionism inspired the experiments of Seurat and his friends. They objected to the complete submission to pure impressions and in its stead reaffirmed the role of intellect. Without ever rejecting any of the basic principles of the Impressionist philosophy, it became their point of departure, a source of new rules and of a new synthesis.

Amid the multiplicity of conflicting tendencies and crosscurrents of late nineteenth-century life, there emerged a drive for renewal, for freedom and discovery. Everything conspired to keep this drive alive and strengthen it. The possibilities of scientific discovery were limitless; it seemed as if science had ceased to be a means to an end; it almost became an end in itself and it also gave new objectives to art. Neo-Impressionism became the symbol of an obsession which held that painting, like physics and chemistry, was capable of infinite progress. It is hardly surprising, therefore, that the literature of Neo-Impressionism should prove as extensive as its illusions.

SEURAT. CAFÉ-CONCERT. 1887. SCHOOL OF DESIGN,
PROVIDENCE, RHODE ISLAND.

SIGNAC AND SEURAT. Signac, in his book *From Dela-croix to Neo-Impressionism* (published in 1889), codified and sim-plified the theories of the movement. When Chevreul developed his law of colors, he concluded that the juxtaposition of two

CÉZANNE.
MONT SAINTE-VICTOIRE
FROM THE LAUVES.
1904-1906.
KUNSTHAUS, ZURICH.

In a letter written to his son in September, 1906, Cézanne said: "There, on the banks of the river (the Arc) the motifs multiply: the same motif, seen from a different angle, offers a subject for study of the greatest interest and so varied that I think I could occupy myself for months without changing my position, leaning sometimes to the right, sometimes to the left." Mont Sainte-Victoire, a subject to which he returned again and again, was for Cézanne the geometric motif he needed, an ideal conjunction of color and form.

complementary colors heightened their intensity, that every object brightens if placed against a shadow, and, conversely, that an object appears darker if placed against something light. A group of young artists—Angrand, Dubois-Pillet, Hippolyte Petitjean, H. E. Cross, Signac, and Seurat—decided to expand and test all the aspects of this theory. All of them claimed to be Impressionists, but theirs was a purely formal acknowledgment. Although they, like their predecessors, rejected local color, they also turned against too free and emotional a method of expression. They evolved a new technique—the juxtaposition of small dots of primary colors— a technique which demanded carefully controlled execution and strict discipline. Signac called himself a great admirer of Monet. But actually, how much common ground was there between the spontaneous expression of the older Impressionists with their love for the fleeting effect, and the intellectual, contrived approach and static sternness of this new group ? These two groups had nothing in common; there was only a seeming relationship which misled the well-meaning Pissarro, always receptive to the experimentation of younger artists, to wax enthusiastic over this new approach in a letter he wrote to Durand-Ruel in 1886. But Pissarro was not a man who would long follow a technique which subjugated impression to a scientific system. Even the name which this new group gave itself—Neo-Impressionists (they also called them-selves "chromoluminarists")— paid homage to the fight of their predecessors for the liberation of painting.

"The Neo-Impressionist painters," Signac wrote, "are those who introduced and developed the so-called technique of Divi-sionism after 1886 through the use of an optical blending of color tones and tints. . . . Neo-Impressionism is not Pointillist but Divisionist. Divisionism unites all the advantages of luminosity, coloration, and harmony: first, by the optical blending of pure color pigments (all the colors of the prism and their tones); second,

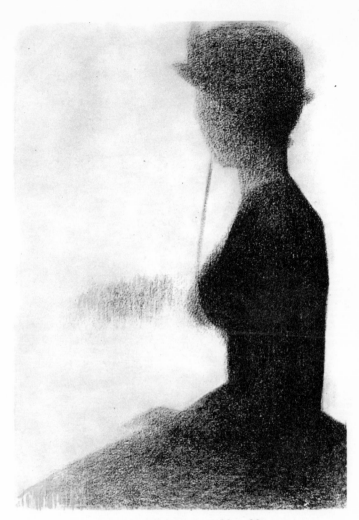

SEURAT. GIRL WITH AN UMBRELLA. 1884-1885.
MUSEUM OF MODERN ART, NEW YORK.

by the separation of the various components (local color, color of light, their interrelation); third, by the balance of these components and their proportions (according to the laws of *contrast, gradation, and irradiation*); and fourth, through the application of brush

DEGAS. THE TOILET. NASJONALGALLERIET, OSLO.

"Painting is one's private life." Thus, in his studies of women, whom he
distorted like mysterious and vaguely hostile mechanisms, Degas revealed
his true feelings, those of a misogynist and bachelor. *"It is the human
animal busy with herself,"* he said to George Moore as he showed him his
sketches, *"a cat licking herself.* Hitherto the nude has always been represented in poses which assumed the presence of an audience, but these women
of mine are honest, simple folk, concerned with nothing else than their
physical condition. Here is another ; she is washing her feet. It is as if
you had looked through a keyhole." One feels ill at ease in front of this too

intimate perfection of the features, this analysis which seeks to be objective
when in reality it is passionate. It was Degas himself who declared:
"A picture is something which demands just as much knavery, malice, and
vice as the perpetration of a crime ; falsify and add a touch of nature."
Pastels are a precious, worldly, elegant technique, well suited to the transience
of the thing seen. But here we are far from the appealing charm of the
eighteenth-century portrait painters. This naturalism grates, and the
attitudes of women washing themselves, drying themselves, and combing their
hair in which Degas persisted in his representation of the human body are
the secret and pitiful avowals of a solitary man devoid of all kindly feelings.

DEGAS. AFTER THE BATH, WOMAN DRYING HER NECK. 1898.
LOUVRE, PARIS.

strokes proportionate to the size of the canvas. The method outlined in these four points governs the use of color by the Neo-Impressionists, though most of them also make use of the more mysterious laws governing the harmony and order of lines and directions. Armed with this knowledge of line and color, the artist can determine the linear and color composition of his painting and coordinate the dominant direction, tone, and color characteristics with the subject."

Thus, the Neo-Impressionists in their naïveté thought that science could postulate the laws of infallible and universal beauty. In 1880, David Sutter had published an important series of articles on "The Phenomena of Vision" in *L'Art* which read almost like an advance program of Neo-Impressionism. "Despite their absolute characters, rules interfere neither with spontaneity of invention nor with execution; science frees the artist of all uncertainty; it permits him to move freely within a very wide circle. Therefore, it is a insult to both art and science to believe that the one necessarily excludes the other." This analysis did not constitute a rejection of Impressionism. It merely expressed the desire to transform an empirical method into a rational and scientific system with ideal and universal beauty as its inevitable end result.

Ever since his early youth, Seurat had been enthusiastic about this discovery. While at the École des Beaux-Arts, he became more and more engrossed in these problems, carried away by the new perspectives which seemed to open up to painting. In 1890, one year before his death, Seurat published a sober and precise analysis of his theory of art. Signac's Neo-Impressionist catechism of 1899 leaned heavily upon Seurat's exposition. Save for one important factor, Signac's work takes everything into account. The only point he fails to mention is that genius sometimes proves stronger than any theoretical system a painter may impose upon himself, that genius may rule a system. As far as Seurat was

SEURAT. LA GRENOUILLÈRE. SCHOOL OF DESIGN, PROVIDENCE, RHODE ISLAND.

concerned, the rigidities imposed by a set of narrowly defined rules proved a blessing. Seurat—that serious, austere, hard-working man—required this sort of constraint. It enabled him to achieve an ideal, almost mystical expression of the absolute he sought to encompass. Seurat had the air of an initiate who, with the help of technical and automatic devices, entered the realm of dreams, of the unreal and unforeseen, like a medium in a state of trance reacting to the emanations of a dream.

Signac—a "wild colorist"— escaped the dangers of a system of rules in his own fashion. His temperament protected him against the consequences of a narrow formalism. But these dangerous games, these "exercises with compass, T-square, and plumb line," frightened many students whose seriousness was greater than their inspiration. "They shut themselves off as in the narrowest prison," wrote Émile Bernard, "doing their lessons and assignments as if their art were a punishment and a trade. There seems to be but one way of doing things: to plan a drawing like a diagram and fill in the various sections with the complementary colors and varying amounts of white." But Félix Fénéon, who wrote an important article on the new school in the *Revue Bruxelloise* published by Octave Maus and Émile Verhaeren, did not share Bernard's opinion. "Is it still necessary," he asked, "to emphasize that this uniform, almost abstract method does not affect an artist's originality; that, perhaps, it even serves it ? It would be idiotic to confuse Pissarro, Dubois-Pillet, Signac, and Seurat. Each of these artists underlines his individuality imperiously, even if only through his own interpretation of the emotional value of color, through his degree of visual sensibility. . . . For them, objective reality is merely the theme for the creation of a higher, sublimated reality transfused with their own personality." And, as a matter of fact, the best of the Neo-Impressionists took extraordinary liberties in the application of the scientific principles of their leader, and that which was to have been an absolute technique soon turned into a method which each and every one of them adapted to his personal inspiration. Lucie Cousturier composed each of her canvases like a decorative mosaic. Maximilian Luce, with his extensive use of soft half-tones, remained the most romantic of Impressionists. His work could never be mistaken for that of Cross, whose emphatic brush strokes and color contrasts foreshadowed the Fauves.

But where artificiality becomes a substitute for inspiration, paint-

GAUGUIN. RIDERS ON THE BEACH. 1902. FOLKWANG MUSEUM, ESSEN.

*"Gauguin painted a small canvas with the sweep of an immense fresco.
From that we culled the wise maxim that every picture should be orna-
mental. . . . He was, for our corrupt times, a sort of Poussin without
classical culture, who, instead of going to Rome to devote himself in serenity
to the study of the old masters, sought feverishly to discover a tradition
behind the crude archaism of the Breton calvaries and the Maori idols. . . .
But, like Poussin, he had a passionate love of simplicity and clarity ; he
inspired in us a striving for freedom of style, and for him, also, synthesis
and style were almost synonymous."* Maurice Denis.

ing must suffer. Gauguin had warned against "the little young chemists of painting who amass small dots. . . the complementary colors which clash but do not harmonize." And Renoir said:

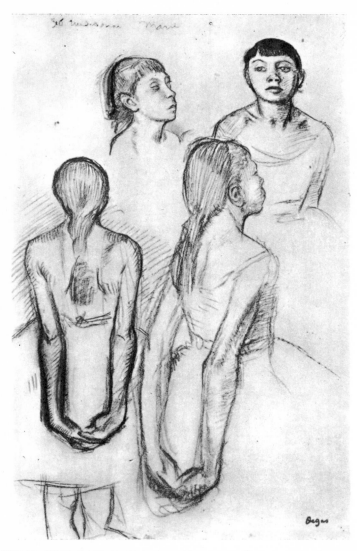

DEGAS. FOUR STUDIES FOR THE SCULPTURE 'THE LITTLE DANCER
AGED FOURTEEN'. 1880. CABINET DES DESSINS, LOUVRE, PARIS.

TOULOUSE-LAUTREC. THE FLYING TRAPEZE. 1899.

"There is something in painting which defies definition and which is the essence of painting.   You confront nature with theories, but nature devastates them all. . . .   The truth of the matter is that in painting, as in all the other arts, there exists no process, however

SEURAT. THE HAUNTED HOUSE. C.1880.

minor, which can be made into a formula." In a letter addressed to Henri van de Velde, Pissarro confessed to having erred: "In view of four years' experience with this theory, which I gave up

REDON. WILD FLOWERS IN A LONG-NECKED VASE. C. 1912.
LOUVRE, PARIS.

"*Flowers, sprung from the banks of two met streams, representation and memory.   Here is the soil of art itself, the good soil of reality, harrowed and plowed by the mind.*"   Redon.

with no little difficulty. . . . I cannot join those Neo-Impressionists who sacrifice movement and life to an aesthetic diametrically opposed to movement and life; perhaps this can be done by one temperamentally suited to this, but I, who wish to escape all narrow theory, cannot do this.˙ . . . After I (and I speak only for myself) discovered the impossibility of capturing the fleeting, superb effects of nature, the impossibility of investing my drawings with a special character, I had to give up. It was high time."

Van Gogh had a clear picture of the future of this movement. He drew a valid conclusion in a letter he wrote his brother Theo from Arles: "Painting, as it is today, promises to become more subtle, more musical, less architectural; above all, it holds forth the promise of color. Let us hope it keeps this promise. . . . As for Pointillism, I consider it a real revolution in the reproduction of halo and similar effects; but it can already be seen that this technique, like all others, cannot become a universal dogma. Still another reason why Seurat's *Grande Jatte* and Signac's broadly patterned landscapes will, as time goes on, become even more personal, more original. . ." But the true worth of every revolution lies in the essentials that posterity will retain and develop; and thus Cubism was to revive most successfully the systematized contrasts of Seurat's *Une Baignade*.

THE LEGACY OF IMPRESSIONISM

THE French poet De Vigny once said that one should love the things one will never see again—a sentiment which found expression in the works of the Impressionists. To capture the mood of the hour or the moment, the fleeting impression—this was the goal and the inimitable heritage of Impressionism. But this imperative of sensation already contained the seeds of the decline of the West or, at least, the seeds of a change in the traditional Western, particularly Latin, conception of man. A universe dominated by patches of light no longer had any room for man, traditionally the focal point of French painting. Impressionism knew only one ideal: light. Cézanne, Renoir, Seurat, and Gauguin owed their discovery of light and color to Impressionism, but in order to rediscover the world of emotion and thought they had to break away from Impressionism. They knew that despite all illusion of change created by light, form remains stable, and, unlike Monet, they affirmed the permanence of this stable world.

Impressionism was not an art of the studios. The escape into open air, into the enchantment and stimulation of nature, should be no more than a means. But Impressionism made it an end in itself, and that is where it erred. The artist needs the solitude of the studio in order to absorb and interpret the emotions experienced when he is face to face with his subject, to arrive at an emotional balance without which there can be no art. Art is translation and needs a dictionary. Nature is that dictionary,

If Théophile Gautier is to be believed, Quentin Metsys had a pavilion built for him in the center of a lake, and there he painted "in order to preserve the perfection of color." Monet, who had had a studio boat built for himself in Argenteuil so that he could work on the Seine, did the same when, after settling at Giverny, he diverted the course of the Epte and made it flow through his garden. The silent pool with its radiant water lilies was his final refuge. He could hardly any longer see that flower of Mallarmé "which grows alone and knows no movement other than its shadow in the still water." The Haystacks *and the* Cathedrals *had been exercises ; the time for meditation had come and with it the right to go beyond observation, to the point of ultimate transpositions. A new world, magical and inexpressible, was born, which painting has yet to exhaust.*

MONET. WATER-LILIES. C. 1916. KUNSTHAUS, ZURICH.

BONNARD. LE PONT DE GRENELLE. 1919. G. RENAND COLLECTION, PARIS.

"Basically I am an Impressionist who, in a century in love with intellectualism and formal abstraction, relies only on the surprise of sensation and the magic of color," said Bonnard. It follows that he can be criticized on the same grounds as Monet and his friends: weakness of form, dispersion of color, and lack of construction. Such criticism does not take sufficient account of the highly creative fantasy of his interplay of colors. Admittedly, nature remained the source of his inspiration, but his reinvention of reality is so ingenious that it is impossible to find the "little sensation" of the Impressionists which was at the source of his canvases. It is the artist and the artist alone who is in control.

but once the words have been committed to memory, the dictionary should no longer be consulted.

When Monet, the last surviving member of his generation, died in 1926, Impressionism was nothing but a memory of something which once had been. What, if anything, had survived? True, the Impressionists gained renown, but theirs was a bitter fame, since they came to believe that they had gone astray, that Impressionism, now accepted by officialdom, had been a monumental delusion. Even today, the general public admires Impressionist art largely for its charm, its freshness, its pleasant and airy qualities—rather than for its pictorial content.

The Impressionists had made their choice between Delacroix's contention that everything in nature was reflection and Ingres' admonition that reflection was only a humble man of little breeding who always stood at the fringe of a crowd, hat in hand, ready to depart. The conflict between these two approaches to painting had to lead to a debate on the purely plastic versus all the other attributes of the object. A round object is not per se an apple. As a matter of fact, all that the Impressionists accomplished in their use of reflection was to disintegrate volume; their successors rebelled and sided with Ingres. But this recognition of values which, briefly, had been shelved did not mean a return to obsolete conceptions, to old forms; it merely helped to justify and introduce the creation of a new order.

Impressionism gave birth to two divergent movements: one stemming from Monet, Van Gogh, and Gauguin, in which painting became a passionate personal expression; this led to the dynamism of Matisse on the one hand and to the nonobjective quality of Klee on the other. The second movement began with Cézanne and Seurat and resulted in an abstract concept: impersonal, geometric, seeking to rid nature of everything nonpictorial, it strove for a classical concept.

BONNARD. LANDSCAPE IN THE MIDI. DRAWING.

The Impressionists also had many other magnificent heirs—illegitimate heirs whom they neither knew nor acknowledged. The big retrospective Cézanne Exhibition at the Salon d'Automne of 1907 was a revelation for Picasso, Braque, and Léger who, at that time, were still trying to find themselves. Cézanne probably would have been among the first to disown these wayward children who claimed him as their spiritual father. But, after all, a painter cannot be held responsible for his message, which frequently transcends his own creativity. Cézanne—the man who said, "I am

CROSS. THE WAVE. C. 1907. GINETTE SIGNAC COLLECTION, PARIS.

"*My sensations, because of the nature of my temperament, demand a grammar, a rhetoric, and a logic.*" Thus, the Pointillist method was bound to appeal to a disciple of Seurat and friend of Signac. In his retreat at Le Lavandou, Cross pursued the Neo-Impressionist aesthetic ; but the Northerner inspired by the light of the Midi could not be satisfied with principles. His treatment became more violent and also freer. In the preface of the catalog of his exhibition at Bernheim's in 1907, M. Denis wrote: "For twenty years, Cross has been trying, more passionately than any of us, to recreate the sun. Now he is getting there ; having observed much and thought much, having multiplied experiences and carried theory to its limits, he is getting there by means of substituting more and more the interplay of color for the interplay of light. . . . Like the Old Masters,

204

Cross believes in representing the sun not by discoloration, but by the intensification of the tints and the boldness of the contrasts." Of all the Neo-Impressionists, Cross is the one who uses the most vivid colors and the most striking scale, a realization of the color fantasies that Gauguin strove after. In doing this, he leads right on to the pointillist Fauvism of Matisse and Derain, who worked—the former at Saint-Tropez, in 1904, and the latter at Collioure in 1905—in the immediate vicinity of Signac and Cross. Nonetheless, what distinguishes the Fauves from their elders is that they bring to their use of color and to their divisionist technique an arbitrariness and a violence whose essential aim is the exaltation of color in all its abrupt changes of tonality or its dissonances. It was thus inevitable that they broke away from the old diatonic scale of Chevreul so dear to the Impressionists.

DERAIN. THE PORT OF COLLIOURE. 1905. PIERRE LÉVY COLLECTION, TROYES.

too old and have not accomplished it, and will not be able to accomplish it. I am a primitive at the start of a road I have discovered. . . . I am a beacon, others will come after me"— was the precursor of the Cubists and of the Abstractionists who followed them. Kandinsky wrote: "Impressionism, and especially the work of Cézanne, gave momentum to the age in which we live; all obstacles, all difficulties only serve to accelerate this momentum, and nothing will stay its course." "Sometimes I ask myself," said Léger, "how far painting would be today without Cézanne. I have studied him for a very long time. He has never left me. There has been no end to my explorations and discoveries. Cézanne taught me the love of form and volume, he has taught me to concentrate on drawing. Thus I came to know that these drawings must be exact and never sentimental."

It required the violent impact of Picasso to set fire to the tinderbox and explode it, to reveal the meaning of Cézanne's comment to Émile Bernard: "Nature consists only of pyramids, cylinders, and cones." Cubism, though a collective revolt against Impressionism, remained a slave of its intellectual method, tied to the fetishism of analysis.

Monet could have foreseen neither Abstractionism nor Tachism, neither the lyricism of Bazaine nor that of Tal Coat. But as early as 1896, Kandinsky was able to sense "the miraculous and direct language of color" while looking at Monet's *Haystack* series at a Moscow exhibit. "I had the impression that somehow painting itself was the subject, and I asked myself if one could not continue along this same road still further. Since that time, I have looked at Russian icons differently, that is to say, I have had an eye for the abstract content of art."

Chevreul's famous law which had inspired Seurat subsequently led to Delaunay's simultaneous contrasts, and Mondrian's Neoplasticism harks back to Seurat—via Delaunay's color Cubism.

CÉZANNE. LANDSCAPE. 1880-1885. ART INSTITUTE, CHICAGO.

Impressionism had dissolved the face of nature; this was the first step toward the search for the inner meaning and rhythm of reality.   There is an obvious progression from Van Gogh to the Fauves and from the Fauves to the Blaue Reiter group.

Léger, whose monumental, majestic works seem the opposite of the "little sensation" of the Impressionists, has paid this tribute to the movement: "It is our task to achieve the greatest degree of dynamism with free color and free form.   This *liberation* was begun by the Impressionists.   After centuries of painting in which the big subjects were the framework of pictures, it was the Impressionists who realized that there was such a thing as art for art's sake, that true beauty could be found in the most unassuming and simplest objects.   Above all, they realized that the color of an

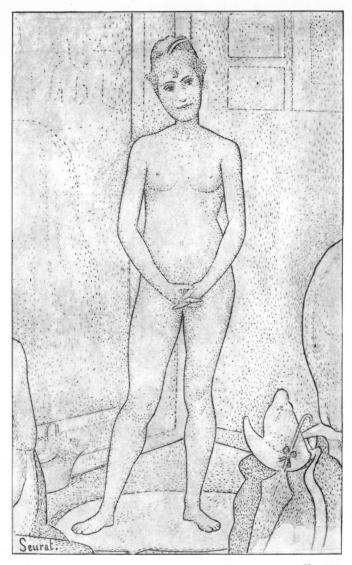

SEURAT. STUDY FOR "LES POSEUSES." 1888.
PRIVATE COLLECTION, PARIS.

object is more important than the object itself. The color of a
landscape, the color of a still life, a figure, a red apple on a green

PICASSO. DANCERS AT REST. 1925.
PRIVATE COLLECTION.

table, became a color composition of red and green.   That was a
revolution and the beginning of that total liberation which enabled

the modern painters of today to develop an art of imagination instead of an art of imitation. . . . Color itself was also liberated; that is to say, before this time we could not, for example, imagine a red existing by itself, not as a part of an object, a material, a human body. Modern artists have liberated color: today a pure red, green, or blue have a *reality* in themselves. Abstract art has made this possible. . . . Today there exists a *new realism,* independent of all imitation and copying of nature. This is the greatest achievement of the last sixty years."

The Impressionists, revolutionaries despite themselves, could not have fathomed the full import of their discoveries. They had liberated instinct, color, and form. Despite their mistakes, despite all the prejudices which they, too, still held, they nonetheless gave emotion, feeling, and thought a specific image, independent of visual expression and representation. That was no minor victory. They discovered the beauty of hitherto unseen worlds. They rediscovered the light which had been lost.

BIOGRAPHIES

BAZILLE. SELF-PORTRAIT.
CABINET DES DESSINS, LOUVRE, PARIS.

BAZILLE, Jean-Frédéric. Born in Montpellier, 1841; died in Beaune-la-Rolande, 1870. Of the Montpellier upper class, he was still a young man when the painter Bruyas, a friend of his parents, introduced him to art. At Bruyas' house he saw works by Corot, Delacroix, and Courbet; especially Courbet made a lasting impression on him. After completion of his secondary education, Bazille obtained permission from his liberal-minded parents to go to Paris to continue his medical studies and, at the same time, attend a painter's studio. At Gleyre's, in 1862, he met Monet, Renoir, and Sisley. His wealth enabled him to lead the life of a fashionable young man, and he was always ready to help his less fortunate friends. Monet took him on a holiday to Chailly in the forest of Fontainebleau, and, in 1864, to Honfleur. Inseparable companions, they shared a studio in the Rue Furstenberg, then one in the Rue de la Paix in Batignolles, and, finally, yet another one in the Rue de la Condamine. When Monet found himself in dire straits, Bazille bought the *Women in a Garden* from him for 2,500 francs; true, he paid in monthly installments of 50 francs, but then a student's purse is not inexhaustible. He was the most discreet of friends, always anxious to help, the good companion who both admired and advised the others. When, in the summer of 1870, the outbreak of the Franco-Prussian War took him by surprise in Montpellier, he enlisted in a regiment of Zouaves. He was killed in battle at Beaune-la-Rolande at the age of twenty-nine. Because his career was broken off so early, Bazille's works are few, but they show a wealth of promise. Less individual than Monet, but equally gifted, he exerted a marked influence on the latter, and it is not unreasonable to suppose that, had he lived, Impressionism after 1870 might have taken a different course.

His two most famous works, *The Family Reunion* and *The Studio*, are reminiscent of Manet in their absence of sculptural qualities, in the similarity of their contrasts, as well as in the rather severe, reserved treatment of composition and color harmonies. A firm, solid, calm style imbues even those subjects which, reproduced with photographic candor, could easily seem pleasantly banal, with true grandeur.

BERNARD, Émile. Born in Lille, 1868; died in Paris, 1941. At the age of sixteen, he spent a year in Cormon's studio as his pupil, albeit a recalcitrant one. Not even the fact that Toulouse-Lautrec was one of his fellow students could influence his negative attitude toward the studio, and he did all that he could to get thrown out. He had seen the work of the Impressionists and, for him, they represented a way of escape. In 1886, he went to Pont-Aven in Brittany where he met Gauguin for the first time. The following year he got to know Van Gogh in Paris; together the two of them went to Asnières in order to paint. But Émile Bernard's style had already become very personal—flat planes of vivid color delineated by black outlines which emphasized their arabesque aspect. This was the style which Gauguin, still a Divisionist in the manner of Pissarro, adopted soon afterwards. There is no longer any doubt about Émile Bernard's influence on Gauguin, but Gauguin, vociferously proclaiming himself the originator of this style, completely eclipsed his young rival. The quarrel that ensued between these two artists was fatal for Bernard, and, in 1891, a frustrated and disillusioned Bernard forsook the path on which he had so promisingly started out. He was then twenty-three years of age. Rather than follow Gauguin in experiments over which he no longer had any control, he made an about-turn, went back to a sombre palette, to chiaroscuro, and strove "to rediscover the former equilibrium of pictorial art." This negative attitude rooted in the past led Bernard toward a hopeless attempt to conciliate his fundamental idealism with a moribund tradition. Like Gauguin, he fled from France and, between 1893 and 1904, aside from short stays in Venice and Spain where he came in contact with Zuloaga, lived mainly in Cairo. He wrote more than he painted (*Réflexions d'un Témoin sur la Décadence du Beau*), founded a review (*La Rénovation Esthétique*), and contributed both to the *Mercure de France* and the review *Occident*. In his poems which he signed with the pseudonym Jean Dorsal, this father of Symbolism displayed a surer creative touch than in his painting. His canvases were highly contrived, and he finally floundered in the series *Grandes étapes de l'Histoire du Monde* where he tried to become a second Michelangelo. Between the work and the

BOUDIN. WOMAN AND CHILD. WATER COLOR. 1865.

program that Bernard set himself there was a vast gulf: "If one does not know to proceed from sensation to intelligence, and from intelligence to supreme reason, one will never discover that spiritual order which is the only thing that can establish harmony among the creations of mankind."

B O U D I N , Eugène.   Born in Honfleur, 1824; died in Deauville, 1898.   The importance which Boudin attributed to working in the open air and "to atmospheric conditions, according to the place, time, and wind" (Baudelaire) explains the influence which he exercised on the young Monet and, through him, on the early stages of Impressionism.   "It is less this world than the element which envelops it that we reproduce," he said.   Originally the proprietor of a small stationery shop in Le Havre, he received encouragement from Millet and, beginning in 1845, he devoted himself to painting.

In 1850, a scholarship enabled him to study in Paris for three years. "Everyone expected that after three years I would return a phoenix in the world of art; I came back more perplexed than ever, feeling the pull of the famous figures of those days; from Rousseau who captivated us, to Corot who was beginning to show us a new road. . . . Gray painting was very little appreciated at that time, especially in seascapes. Gudin reigned; Isabey improved on the coloring of nature. Le Poitevin and others created a furore by painting from memory; this was hardly the time to introduce gray. Nobody wanted it. One was forced to retire to one's own countryside and wait for better days, and that is why I went away for fifteen years without returning to Paris." After his return to Le Havre he worked with Jongkind, with the young Monet whom he initiated into painting in 1862, and with Courbet, who freed him from his timidity. He took part in the first Impressionist exhibition (1874) and, late in life, won some official recognition—a gold medal at the International Exhibition (1889) and the Legion of Honor (1892). But all his friends knew his true worth: "If I have become a painter, I owe it to Eugène Boudin" (Monet); "You are the king of skies" (Corot); "You are a seraphim, there is no one but you who knows the sky" (Courbet). He visited Brittany, Belgium, Holland, and Venice, but for all practical purposes his work rotated around the estuary of the Seine; he loved its silvery beaches, the sea breeze which drives the big clouds whose shadows glide over the water, the little ports with their sails outlined against the sky. "It is now twenty years since I first began to seek that delicacy, that all-pervading charm of light. How fresh it is: it is soft, faded, slightly rose-tinted. The objects dissolve. There is nothing but color values everywhere. The sea was superb, the sky soft and velvety; it later turned to yellow; it became warm and then the setting sun imbued everything with beautiful nuances of bluish-purple. . ."

CAILLEBOTTE, Gustave. Born in Paris, 1848; died in Gennevilliers, 1894. The name of Caillebotte evokes less a painter than a collector, for his powers of discernment were greater than his talent. He had initially frequented Bonnat's studio, had even been admitted to the École des Beaux-Arts in 1873, but he was discouraged from the outset and did not continue. Instead, he devoted himself to marine engineering. He lived at Argenteuil. Monet became his neighbor, introduced him to his friends, and took him with them on their boating parties. Thus Monet introduced him to the movement. It was Caillebotte whom Renoir painted in profile, astride a chair in the foreground of the *Déjeuner des Canotiers*. Timid and reserved himself, he appreciated audacity in others. For them he was providence itself, always buying "what is unsalable" (*The Swing, Le Moulin de la Galette*) and playing an active part in the organization of their exhibitions. Preoccupied with the fate of his collection—he was a bachelor—he made a will in 1876 which left all his pictures to the state on condition that they be hung in the Louvre. Renoir was named as his executor. On his death in 1894, the conditions of the legacy came under dispute. The scandal was considerable, the Institute indignant. Gérôme, the illustrious painter-member of the Institute, threatened to resign: "I do not know these gentlemen and of the donation I know only the title. . . . Are there not some paintings of Monsieur Monet in it ? Of Monsieur Pissarro and others ? For the state to accept such filth would be a blot on morality." Clemenceau intervened. Renoir came to terms with the state and 8 out of 16 Monets, 7 out of 18 Pissarros, 2 out of 4 Cézannes were accepted; these were finally hung in the Louvre—in 1928.

CASSATT, Mary. Born in Pittsburg, Pa., 1845; died in Mesnil-Beaufresne (Oise), 1926. The daughter of a banker, she went to Europe in 1868 to complete the education she had received

at the Pennsylvania Academy and to visit the museums of Italy, Spain, and Belgium.   Very well informed on the world of art, she advised her friend Mrs. Havemeyer to buy the works of Degas. He, who did not know her, noticed her work in the 1874 Salon.   A mutual friend introduced them, and this meeting marked the beginning of a deep friendship; for the first time, Degas abandoned his misogyny.   They shared the feelings common to the class to which they belonged, and yet they had the same scorn for convention. Both were cooly rational, and both preferred drawing to color. At the age of thirty-two, prompted by her desire to break away from the social obligations imposed by her environment as well as by her feeling of artistic vocation, Mary Cassatt devoted herself entirely to painting. She followed the advice of Degas, but the simplification and precision of her line are more reminiscent of Japanese prints. She was an Impressionist in her use of colors and also in the treatment of her themes of motherhood and infancy, of which she painted innumerable series. Living in the heart of the Impressionist movement, she contributed considerably toward making the works of her friends known in America. When Durand-Ruel found himself on the brink of bankruptcy because of the concerted efforts of his fellow art dealers, she lent him money.

CÉZANNE. THE SMOKER. 1890-1892. BOYMANS MUSEUM, ROTTERDAM.

CÉZANNE. THE CARD PLAYERS. C. 1894. LOUVRE, PARIS.

She bought Impressionist paintings both for herself and for her family (her brother was a railroad executive in Pennsylvania) and made her other friends—the Havemeyers of New York, the Stillmans, and the Whittemores—buy them. Practically blind, she died in 1926 in her Château at Mesnil-Beaufresne near Beauvais.

CÉZANNE, Paul. Born in Aix-en-Provence, 1839; died there, 1906. After establishing a comfortable business in the hat trade, his father had become a prosperous banker. Cézanne's career, therefore, seemed mapped out in advance; after a normal secondary

221

education at the Aix lycée, where he made friends with his fellow-pupil Zola, he began to study law. But his feeling for art was overwhelming, and he could no longer ignore the call of his true vocation. This was not in line with the plans of his father, who admonished him with the words: "My son, think of the future ! With genius one may die, with money one can eat." The conflict was the conventional one, but the father finally relented, and Cézanne left for Paris in 1861. There he enrolled at the Académie Suisse, sought the company of Pissarro, and strove to get into the École des Beaux-Arts. Oddly enough, the reason for his rejection was: "Cézanne has the temperament of a colorist. Unfortunately, he paints with violence." Cézanne had looked forward to the re-establishment of the close ties with his old friend Zola, and the increasing coolness of their relationship added to his feeling of dejection. Mortified and helpless, Cézanne returned to Aix. His father made every effort to interest him in his banking business, but on one of the ledgers the young Paul wrote these lines: "Cézanne the banker shudders at what he sees—behind his counter a future painter is being born." Tired of fighting, his father again agreed to send his son to Paris in November, 1862. At the Académie Suisse he found Pissarro once more and was introduced to Guillaumin, Degas, Bazille, Monet, Renoir, and Sisley. But his shyness and modesty made him adopt an expression of fierceness and he made friends only with some difficulty. Also, the power, vehemence, and baroque quality of his painting left people aghast. He was refused a second time at the École des Beaux-Arts (1863) and rejected by the Salon (1866). Paris oppressed him, and during the course of these years he often escaped to Aix to recuperate in the land that suited his fiery temperament so well. He worked extremely hard, nearly always in solitude; he had to teach himself everything, to discover everything, and these self-imposed difficulties exasperated him. When war broke out in 1870, he remained at

Estaque, near Marseilles, and devoted himself to landscape painting. But the course of events had dispersed his friends and, after
the war, rather than return to Paris, he preferred to set himself up in
Auvers-sur-Oise, a small village near Pontoise, where Pissarro was
then living.

His stay in Auvers (1872-1874) proved decisive. Alongside
Pissarro, he acquired the discipline which had been so lacking, the
economy of means and the equilibrium necessary for inspiration
and execution. Converted to Impressionism, he took up painting
in the open air; his palette became brighter, his touch was no
longer heavy, as if laid on with the knife, but restrained, regular,
and delicate. His logical mind, however, demanded a greater
discipline than the pseudo-analytical approach of Monet. He
aspired toward a more syntheticized and constructive vision,
of which the basic elements would be the sphere, the cylinder,
and the cone. He made contact again with his painter friends
and, in 1874, participated in their first exhibition at Nadar's, where
he showed three pictures, including the *Modern Olympia* and *The
House of the Hanged Man*. At the exhibition which the Impressionist
group organized three years later (1877) in the Rue Le Peletier, he
was represented by sixteen canvases; but, hurt by the hilarity they
provoked, he returned to the solitude of his native countryside,
determined "to make of Impressionism something solid and
lasting, like the art of museums." Each year he made an appearance in Paris so as not to be forgotten, hoping that at some time
he might finally be able to win over the jury. Thanks to the
charitable intervention of Guillemet, he was at last able to announce
to his family that he had been accepted for the Salon of 1882. But
he was aware of the insignificance of this encouragement and,
tired of the machinations and intrigues of the Parisian art world,
he retired to Aix, relinquishing the pursuit of success and, at the
same time, that superficial search after fugitive effects which

satisfied his Impressionist friends. He felt the need for something more serious. He needed truth, not the truth of a transient moment, but a lasting truth which could be apprehended; for at heart, Cézanne, the man of the Mediterranean, was a classicist. Impressionism had burst the bonds of official painting and had rediscovered the vitality of a true tradition. It had, above all, discovered light, and Cézanne never disowned this fundamental contribution. But he meant to go beyond it, to deepen his sensation. He did not want to sacrifice volume and space, but, on the contrary, to accentuate them in simplifying them, and, finally, he wished to achieve the harmony of color within that of form.

After 1889, success arrived slowly. At the International Exhibition he was able to show *The House of the Hanged Man* ; the following year he was invited to exhibit in Brussels. In 1895, Vollard exhibited some 150 works in his shop in the Rue Laffitte. This created a scandal, but Cézanne became aware of the admiration he excited among young painters and young critics—Maurice Denis, Émile Bernard, Gasquet, Jaloux, and Larguier—and his art blossomed under this approval. The truth for which he searched became richer and more complex. Going beyond the geometric synthesis of previous years, he gave himself up to lyricism of form and color which he strove to integrate into his vision of reality. It was a difficult task, by no means lacking in obstacles; it postulated a perfect sincerity with regard to reality as well as with regard to himself. A few days before his death, he was able to write to Émile Bernard: "I am always studying, and it seems to me that I am making slow progress." The retrospective exhibition of 1907 in the *Salon d'Automne* with fifty-six canvases from the Pellerin, Cézanne, and Gangnat collections, was an affirmation of Cézanne's triumph. The Louvre had received some of his works through the Camondo bequest, and these were exhibited there in 1911.

DEGAS. DANCERS AT THE BAR. 1876-1877. METROPOLITAN MUSEUM OF ART, NEW YORK.

CROSS, Henri-Edmond (real name: Delacroix). Born in Douai, 1856; died in Saint-Clair, 1910. His studies at the École des Beaux-Arts in Lille led him to Bonvin's studio in Paris, where he discovered that the black, realistic style he had been taught was merely the semblance of tradition, and that the true tradition was more readily to be found in the discoveries of the Impressionists.

He met Seurat and Signac around 1884, adopted their light-toned palette and, like them, used the stippled brush stroke and divided the tones. It is significant that the technical research into light was carried out by northerners, and in his distinctly methodical fashion Cross pursued his own experiments in the wake of his friends. "In the act of creation, one's will as well as instinct must play a major part, and the will has to have a precise basis. This precision occupies my mind. I look for it in the law of color contrasts. I do not let myself think about it too much; on the contrary, I *believe* that this is what I lack most. If you are endowed with artistic sensibility, the search for, and development of, a method will not prevent you from expressing your own impressions."

A stay in the Midi at Saint-Clair, near Lavandou, and a trip to Italy revealed to him that color cannot reproduce light, but can only provide an equivalent. Thenceforth, his orientation became · more personal. He renounced the optical mixture of colors and avoided gray, for the sun does not lessen but increases the intensity of the tones. The search for contrasts was all that interested him. He was—almost— already a Fauve.

D E G A S , Edgar. Born in Paris, 1834; died there, 1917. "The air that one can see in the work of the old masters is not the air that one breathes." "My art is in no way spontaneous; it is entirely contrived." Thus Degas, who had played a part in the advent of Impressionism and had been one of the principal witnesses to its success, stood opposed to two basic principles of the movement— the necessity of, or almost superstitious belief in, open-air painting, and direct impression. This affirmation of independence, or, more exactly, his rejection of the approval of others, constituted the drama of his life and work. His father was the banker Auguste De Gas and he belonged to the upper reaches of banking society.

Degas, free to direct his life as he chose, decided after an excellent classical education to devote himself to painting and went through his apprenticeship at the École des Beaux-Arts under the direction of Lamothe, a pupil of Ingres and Flandrin (1855). But he would not allow himself to be tied down, and the following year he left for Italy to study the Florentine masters (1856-1860). The works dating from this period, both portraits and compositions, not only show the influence of the Italian sixteenth-century masters, but also a heightened and already individual vision. His feeling for composition and for spontaneous movement led him to the group of painters of the Café Guerbois, and more particularly to Manet, whom he had met in the Louvre. Between them there sprang up a close friendship, often stormy but firmly anchored, which led to a sort of emulation in the choice and utilization of themes borrowed from everyday life: racetracks and café scenes; women washing themselves, brushing their hair, women bathing—themes in which Degas usually found fresh approaches. For it was the unusual motif as much as the original arrangement of the picture that he looked for, as in the *Racecourse* series (begun in 1862), the *Theater* series (begun in 1868), and his ballet pictures, all subjects which were still completely novel. Degas took part in the first Impressionist exhibition in 1874, but he was the only one among them who sacrificed none of the precision of an uncompromising vision, the only one, also, who considered drawing to be the means of expression which best reconciled his love of movement with his love of precision: "I paint with the line." But, paradoxically, when his eyesight deteriorated he was to translate his inner vision in accents of intense color—blues, yellows, and reds—in powerfully juxtaposed brush strokes. He was a perpetual inventor of new techniques, and when threatened with total blindness he gave up pastels for sculpture *(The Little Dancer Aged Fourteen* was shown at the Impressionist exhibition of 1881.) Difficult and independent

GAUGUIN. BRETON VILLAGE IN THE SNOW. 1894. LOUVRE, PARIS.

as he was, he gave his support to Impressionism, yet he remained practically a stranger to the movement. He followed its evolution, making his mark on it and giving advice, but he never personally attended its exhibitions. He was the first person to buy a Gauguin and so, to some extent, the sponsor of the man who was to signal the end of Impressionism. His superior intelligence, his logical and mocking mind, and his intractable character were just as responsible for his isolation as was his infirmity. There remained to him the bitter consolation of being alone among the Ingres, the Delacroix, and the Cézannes of his collection.

G A U G U I N, Paul. Born in Paris, 1848; died in Atuana in the Marquesas Islands, 1903. His father was a journalist of Radical Republican convictions; his mother, born in Peru, was the

daughter of the painter André Chazan and of a Spanish mother—
Flora Tristan, a militant disciple of Saint-Simon and a woman
of letters. Through her, he was descended from the Borgias
d'Aragon, who had been viceroys of Peru. After the *coup d'état* of
1851, the Gauguin family went into voluntary exile to Lima.
Gauguin's mother, having lost her husband, returned to France
with her children after spending four years in Peru. Paul was then
aged seven. Educated in Orléans, he was attracted to the life of
a sailor. He enlisted as an apprentice on a merchant ship, visited
Rio de Janeiro, Bahia, Sweden, and Denmark. After the death of
his mother in 1871 he gave up the sea and became a broker. His
punctuality and seriousness soon procured him an enviable position and gave promise of a future in the world of finance which
would be both brilliant and assured—just what was required to
win the heart of the young Danish woman, Mette-Sophie Gad,
whom he married in 1873. He had a fine bourgeois household,
five children, social life, money. But one of the employees of the
bank, a man by the name of Schuffenecker, used to devote his
spare time to painting and induced Gauguin to follow his example:
it was an agreeable Sunday pastime which came to absorb him more
and more. He showed a landscape at the Salon of 1876 and slowly
amassed pictures by Jongkind, Manet, Renoir, Monet, Pissarro,
and Sisley. He spent 15,000 francs on building up a collection of
Impressionist works. Pissarro advised him and introduced him
to Cézanne as well as to the rest of the group. Gauguin exhibited
with them on several occasions—in 1880, 1881, 1882, and 1886.
He was still looked on as an amateur but, in the autumn of 1883, he
gave up the bank and moved with his wife and children to Rouen
where Pissarro lived. Full of ambition, he assumed that his work
would enable him to lead a life of ease. But he sold nothing, and
his savings were soon exhausted. His wife became exasperated
and, worn out, took him to Denmark in 1884 in the hope of bring-

ing him back to an outlook more in conformity with the bourgeois norm. An exhibition in Copenhagen was a failure; Gauguin abandoned his family, except for his son Clovis, and returned to Paris in 1885. To keep himself alive he became a billposter.

Soon afterwards, escaping from the city, he went to Brittany in 1886 and took up residence at an inn in Pont-Aven frequented by painters from the Cormon studio and the Académie Julian. There he kept to himself, a focal point of curiosity for all. When he returned to Paris, he made friends with Van Gogh, visited Degas, and planned a trip to the tropics. In the spring of 1887, he embarked for Martinique, but returned the following year, completely penniless, and once more took refuge in Pont-Aven. Then, summoned by Van Gogh, he went to Arles. But the visit to Provence ended tragically and Gauguin returned to Paris. At the Café Volpini his work was included in "An Exhibition of Paintings of the Impressionist and Synthesist Groups" and he exhibited in Brussels with *Les Vingt*. In 1891, he left for Tahiti to live "in ecstasy, in peace, and in art," and strove to rid himself of everything that was not elemental. "For me, Barbary is a restorer of youth." In 1893, he exhibited his Tahitian works at Durand-Ruel's; they created considerable interest, particularly among the younger generation—Bonnard, Vuillard, and the Nabis. Having broken with the Impressionists, he returned to Tahiti in 1895, lived his legend and, despite illness, misery, and ridiculous squabbles with the local authorities, never stopped producing masterpieces. Penniless and embittered, his health completely broken, he died in the Marquesas Islands on May 8, 1903.

GONZALÈS, Éva. Born in Paris, 1849; died there, 1883. She came of a cultured background, receptive to the arts, and it was only natural that her family, becoming aware of her talent, should put her under the tutelage of the painter Chaplin. Her small studio in the Rue Breda was near Manet's, a fact which gave rise to a certain amount of talk. Famous men surrounded by an aura of scandal exercise a fascinating attraction on innocent young ladies. Alfred Stevens, a friend of the Gonzalès', introduced Manet to them. Éva became his pupil and worked assiduously in close contact with him during 1869. Manet was enchanted by Éva's beauty and intelligence. She, on her part, admired the genius of her master. She adopted his mannerisms, and her painting might almost be said to be a poeticized version of Manet. She learned to simplify and to reject everything that was not essential. But she stiffened instinctively in the face of Impressionism. Her obstinacy was undoubtedly due in part to the fact that Manet was introduced to the new theories by another charming young woman who might have proved a rival. But she did not. Berthe Morisot married Eugène Manet, and Éva Gonzalès married their mutual friend Henri Guérard, a collector of etchings. He, who lived on the fringe of the movement and was more concerned with his collection than with living art, no doubt warned his young wife against all modernist tendencies. At the 1879 Salon, she exhibited a number of canvases which affirmed her taste for interior scenes. But was she aware of being on the wrong track ? She seemed to return to Impressionism, used both more lively colors and a bolder touch. In 1883, at the age of thirty-four, she died in childbirth.

G U I L L A U M I N, Armand. Born in Paris, 1841; died there, 1927. "He is an architect of the great future ahead and a good fellow of whom I am very fond," said Cézanne. The two men had met at the Académie Suisse through Pissarro, and they formed a little group which always remained united. Forced to earn his living as an employee of the railways, Guillaumin devoted his free Sundays to painting and often went to Auvers-sur-Oise to join his friends gathered at the house of Doctor Gachet. He took part in the first Impressionist exhibition in 1874 and remained one of the few faithfuls whose work was still to be seen at the last exhibition of 1886. He was, in fact, immune to external influences and thus preserved his very direct and personal vision, though its realism did not always succeed in eliminating vulgarity. In 1891, he won a 100,000-franc prize in a lottery which enabled him to devote his time entirely to painting. His landscapes of the Creuse and Holland (1904) give an impression of virile authority, an illusion created by the intensity of color, but one which did not always succeed in concealing a lack of discipline.

JONGKIND, Johan Barthold. Born in Latrop, Holland, 1819; died in La Côte-Sainte-André, near Grenoble, 1891. The eighth child of a Dutch pastor, Jongkind met the landscape painter Isabey at The Hague; Isabey took him as a pupil and, in 1846, sent him to Paris to complete his studies. A bohemian to the core, an alcoholic, always in debt, he suffered from a feeling of persecution. In 1858, he gained some measure of stability when, in Paris, he met a Dutch woman who helped him and took him with her on her visits to Nivernais and La Côte-Saint-André in the Dauphiné. Heedless of everything which did not immediately satisfy his instinctive genius, his work was uneven, hasty, and disappointing. His oil paintings at their best are in the tradition of the great Dutch landscape painters—Ruysdael and Van Goyen in particular. Nevertheless, this was not enough to make him an Impressionist, any more than the fact that he was one of the first foreign painters of the School of Paris. But his water colors and his drawings are a completely different matter: able to capture the most fleeting of sensations, he had that rapidity of execution and sureness of touch which the Impressionists in turn strove to attain.

MANET, Édouard. Born in Paris, 1832; died there, 1883. The son of a senior official at the Ministry of Justice and of the daughter of a diplomat, he was sent to boarding school in Vaugirard in 1839 and then to the Collège Rollin, completing his secondary education in 1848. Then he had to choose a career. "You will study law," his father said. But Manet wanted to be a painter. It then was decided that he was to become a naval officer, and he went to sea as an apprentice sailor. A voyage to Rio de Janeiro did not change Manet's mind about his artistic vocation; if anything, it was strengthened and he had to be allowed to do what he wanted. His father gave way and Édouard enrolled at the studio of Thomas Couture in 1850, where, despite the incompatibility of master and pupil, he remained for nearly six years. From his liaison with Suzanne Leenhoff was born a son, Léon Édouard (1852), who was presented to his family as the young woman's younger brother. In 1863, after the death of his father, Manet married her. His was the easy-going life of a well-off young man and he visited Holland, Germany, and Italy in 1856. The first picture he submitted to the Salon of 1859—the *Absinthe Drinker*—was rejected; but in 1861, the *Spanish Guitar Player* was accepted and given honorable mention. However, the official career of which he dreamed was closed to him. *Lola de Valence, Jeune Femme Couchée en Costume Espagnol* and *Concert in the Tuileries Gardens,* all of which were exhibited at Martinet's in 1863, caused a scandal. At the *Salon des Refusés,* the *Déjeuner sur l'Herbe* was taken as a gesture of defiance. It was almost certainly in order to appease the jury that Manet, in the years following, sent in the *Angels at the Tomb of Christ* and *Christ Insulted by the Soldiers,* but he again compromised himself with his *Olympia* (1865). The critics vented their wrath and, despite the congratulations of Baudelaire, Manet, discouraged, went off to Spain. The hostility of the general public and the ostracism of the jury had made him the leader of a school despite himself, and official honors were henceforth out of the question. At the time of the International Exhibition of 1867 he had a pavilion erected at his own expense in the Place de l'Alma; there he showed all his rejected canvases. "Husbands took their wives to the Pont de l'Alma. Everyone wanted to seize this unique opportunity to split his sides in laughter." In 1868, however, the Salon accepted the *Portrait of Zola* and the following year the *Déjeuner à l'Atelier* and *The Balcony.* Manet's family was dispersed by the war, and he himself enlisted as a lieutenant in the General Staff of the National Guard. After the end of the war he set himself up in the Rue de Saint-Petersbourg, where his studio became a meeting-place for his friends: Mallarmé, Antonin Proust, Chabrier, Clemenceau, and pretty young women.

He refused to take part in the Impressionist exhibition at Nadar's in 1874, but, under the influence of his pupil Berthe Morisot (who had become his sister-in-law), he allowed himself to be taken to Genevilliers and to Argenteuil where he painted *The Monet Family in the Garden.* He seemed to have been won over to the Impressionist aesthetic and it was in this style that he painted the *Grand Canal* of Venice in 1875. The Salon turned him down in 1876 and 1877, when he submitted *Le Linge* and *Nana ;* in 1878, he gave up the attempt, but never the hope, of winning over the official world of art. Naïvely, he proposed to the Prefect of the Seine to paint a series of compositions on the theme of Paris— the market, railways, and the Métro. However, struck down by locomotor ataxy, he was forced to pay attention to his health; he took a cure at Bellevue, stayed at Versailles, and worked on *Le Bar aux Folies-Bergère* (1881); finally, thanks to his friend Antonin Proust, who had become Minister of Fine Arts, he was awarded the Legion of Honor. But illness undermined his strength and, on April 30, 1883, he died. He had never really known the glory which he craved—a glory amply confirmed by his posthumous exhibition at the École des Beaux-Arts in 1884.

M O N E T , Claude. Born in Paris, 1840; died in Giverny, 1926. The son of Le Havre shopkeepers, it was there that he spent his childhood and youth. By the time he was fifteen he was already well-known for his caricatures; he was "a personality in the town"; his portrait-caricatures sold for twenty francs apiece and caught the attention of Boudin (1858). The latter made friends with the young artist and took him into the countryside to initiate him into landscape painting. Boudin's influence was decisive, and on his advice Monet went to Paris in 1859, where, for a short while, he worked at the Académie Suisse with Pissarro; but most of his time was spent in discussions at the Brasserie des Martyrs. Conscripted in 1860, he spent two years in Algeria; but a bout of typhoid fever cut short his military service. He rejoined Boudin and Jongkind at Le Havre, then returned to Paris in 1862 to enroll in the studio of Gleyre, where he made friends with Bazille, Renoir, and Sisley. His love of independence revolted against the formalism of the École and he took his friends with him to Chailly in the forest of Fontainebleau (1863), and to Honfleur (1864). Together they discovered the peaceful horizons of the Ile-de-France, the charm of the banks of the Seine at Ville-d'Avray and Bougival; they frequently escaped into Normandy, to Trouville, Sainte-Adresse, and Étretat. At the Salon of 1866 he exhibited the portrait of *Camille,* but he was not as successful with the *Woman in a Garden,* which was rejected by the jury of the 1867 Salon. His material situation was precarious and constantly deteriorating. Tempted to commit suicide, it was the friendship of Bazille which saw him through, despite a new setback at the 1869 Salon. When war was declared he went first to Trouville, then to London, where he found Pissarro once more and made the acquaintance of Durand-Ruel. He then went to Holland, where his landscapes acquired his typical luminous colors.

On his return he went to live in Argenteuil in 1872-1878, where, in 1873, he built himself a studio boat like Daubigny's "Botin" from which he could observe the incessant interplay of light and water. He again took up the project which Bazille had envisaged of grouping friends into a society and of giving a joint exhibition of their work. This took place in 1874, at Nadar's, and Monet showed his *Impression, Sunrise.* This exhibit was the official baptism of Impressionism, and Monet was recognized as the leader of the group. But financial difficulties continued and he lived on loans. Chocquet, at critical moments, played a providential role

and bought canvases at 40 to 50 francs apiece (1877). Perhaps inspired by Turner, Monet was fascinated by themes which had never been touched before, such as the Gare Saint-Lazare, the railway bridge at Argenteuil, the banks of the Seine at Vétheuil, sacrificing the subject to a study of the changing effects of light. In 1883, he went to live in Giverny which remained his favorite home for the rest of his days, though he still went on visits to Bordighera with Renoir (1884), to Haarlem, to Belle-Ile-en-Mer (1886), to Antibes (1888), and elsewhere. From 1890 until the end of his life he was preoccupied with a variety of themes on which he worked unceasingly. During this period, he produced those amazing series which are the affirmation of all his visionary talent; the *Haystacks* (1890); the *Poplars,* followed by the *Cathedrals* (1893-

1894); and then, between 1901 and 1904, the *Water Lilies* and the *Banks of the Thames*; and finally, in 1908, the *Views of Venice*. Having retired to Giverny, making only very rare appearances in Paris, the supreme master of Impressionism died in 1926, having been a part both of its triumph and of its ultimate decline.

M O R I S O T , Berthe. Born in Bourges, 1841; died in Paris, 1895. Her well-to-do father was a prefect under Louis-Philippe. The bourgeois tradition made allowances for everything except for genius. However, Berthe Morisot, without in any way renouncing her background or her deepest aspirations, succeeded in being both a perfect housewife and a painter. When she was fifteen, she and her sister began to take drawing lessons. This was part of a young girl's education and her family was pleased with the appro-bation of her professors. Full of ambition, she went to work in the Louvre, studying Raphael, and there she met Fantin-Latour and Manet, who made her aware of the inadequacy of her teaching. She then studied with Corot, who was amazed at her talent and lent her canvases to copy. She exhibited at the Salon of 1864. But it was Manet who revealed her to herself. He asked her to pose for *The Balcony,* and through him she discovered that a picture must be built up by means of rhythm, calculation, and selection. She realized that her art was superficial even if the touch was inspired; therefore she started painting portraits, which demand a greater discipline. There are unquestionable similarities between the work of Berthe Morisot and that of Manet, but this is due more to a similarity of subject than to any real influence. The master, who was so susceptible to feminine charm, acknowledged the ascen-dancy of his pupil, and his palette, which was still somber, became more luminous under her influence.

After 1872, Berthe Morisot's style broadened and achieved its equilibrium in a true harmony of color and light. In 1874 she married Eugène Manet, the handsome, bearded talker of the *Déjeuner sur l'Herbe*. The comradeship between Manet and Berthe Morisot became a delightful friendship of brother-in-law and sister-in-law. Freed by marriage from the constraining bonds of family prejudice, she gave up striving after official approbation and exhibited at Nadar's in the first Impressionist exhibition. Renoir, Mallarmé, Degas, Monet, Caillebotte, and Whistler were all welcome at her home. Her subjects belonged to her own peaceful world—the faces of children, interiors, and open-air scenes. After 1884, her stylistic evolution proceeded logically toward a more generous and firmer treatment of line. She was deeply stricken by her husband's death in 1892 and her work began to suffer. She developed a broader style, less firm and well-constructed. Her emotions seemed to defeat her craftsmanship. Light suffused form and dissolved it. In the case of Berthe Morisot, this prime weakness of Impressionism was intensified by a feminine sensibility. Berthe Morisot died on March 2, 1895.

P I S S A R R O , Camille Jacob. Born in Saint-Thomas in the Antilles, 1830; died in Paris, 1903. Sent to Paris to study at the age of twelve, he afterwards returned to the Antilles to work in his father's hardware business; ultimately, his family accepted the fact that he wanted to be an artist and permitted him to return to Paris. He arrived there at the time of the 1855 International Exhibition and discovered Ingres, Delacroix, Courbet, and Corot; it was the last-named who exerted a decisive influence upon Pissarro, who never ceased to acknowledge his indebtedness. In 1859, at the Académie Suisse, he met Monet and, two years later, Cézanne and Guillaumin. In 1866 he went to live in Pontoise, and in 1869 he established himself at Louveciennes. In 1870, in face of the Prussian advance, he fled to Brittany and then to London, where he married Julie Vellay, the mother of his children. There he also

MONET. RUE MONTORGUEIL, FÊTE OF 30 JUNE. 1878.
MADAME LINDON COLLECTION, PARIS.

PISSARRO. BOULEVARD MONTMARTRE AT NIGHT. 1897. NATIONAL GALLERY, LONDON.

met Durand-Ruel, who bought two of his canvases, and Monet, who, like himself, was a refugee. When he returned to Louveciennes, the Prussians had ransacked his studio and destroyed nearly fifteen hundred canvases.

From 1872 to 1884 he lived in Pontoise and gathered around him Cézanne, Guillaumin, and Vignon, and it was he who brought Cézanne to Impressionism and helped him rid himself of his "somber manner." Thanks to Durand-Ruel, he began to become known and was pleasantly astonished to see one of his own pictures

sell for 950 francs in a public auction.   In 1874, he took part in
the first Impressionist exhibition and insisted that Cézanne, whom
he never ceased to encourage, should also be admitted.   Talented
young men were continually benefiting from his unending kind-
ness; he helped them in their experiments and put up with the
enthusiasm of Gauguin, Signac, Seurat, and Van Gogh.   At one
time he even experimented with Pointillism, but he soon discarded
so rigid a system.   After 1884, he retired to Éragny, near Gisors,
where he painted gardens and orchards in bloom, and he paid visits
to Rouen (1896-1898), Dieppe, and Le Havre.   From 1893 until
his death he painted views of Paris which, with their plunging
vistas of the boulevards and their range of light effects, constituted a series which even Monet might have envied.   "If one
examines Pissarro's art in its entirety," wrote Gauguin in 1902,
"one finds, despite its unevenness, not only an intense instinct for
art which never contradicts itself, but also an art which is essentially intuitive in the best tradition.   He copied everyone, you
say ?   Why not ?   Everyone copied him, but denied him.   He
was one of my masters and I do not deny him."

REDON, Odilon.   Born in Bordeaux, 1840; died in Paris,
1916.   Although he belonged to the Impressionist generation,
Odilon Redon was, in fact, a man apart.   Too intelligent not to
be independent, he found the Impressionist movement a little
"dull-witted."   Bresdin, whom he had known at Bordeaux and
who initiated him into the art of engraving, had helped him to
discover the importance of the extrasensory world: "True art lies
in the apprehended reality."   The imagination of the artist cannot
create in a void, it depends essentially on the attentive observation
of the real, even when it evokes a world of fantasy, indeed of the
demoniac.   "I have always felt the need to copy nature in the
form of small, specific, accidental objects.   Is is only after expend-

RENOIR. THE JUDGMENT OF PARIS. 1908-1910. PHILLIPS COLLECTION, WASHINGTON.

ing every effort of will to achieve a minutely accurate representation of a blade of grass, a stone, a branch, or a section of an old wall, that I am driven as in torment to create something imaginary. External nature, thus apprehended and determined, becomes, in transformation, my source and my catalyst; it is to the moments following such exercises that I owe my best works." Redon's life, uneventful and filled with hard work, furnishes the biographer with but few interesting stories. It was Mallarmé's friendship which, after 1886, finally helped to achieve recognition of his work—an exact pictorial parallel of the experiments of the Symbolist poets.   But it was not until after his death that Redon, who had already exercised an influence on the Nabis, was fully recognized.   Later he was even hailed by the Surrealists as one of their earliest precursors.

R ENOIR , Pierre Auguste.   Born in Limoges, 1841; died in Cagnes, 1919.   Renoir was the son of a poor tailor.   In 1845, the family went to live in Paris.   He attended the elementary school, and at the age of thirteen he was apprenticed to a painter of chinaware.   He decorated vases.   His employer convinced his parents that he should be allowed to attend evening art classes and, whenever he had a spare moment, he went to the Louvre.   He was determined to be a painter but, so as not to be a burden to his family, he saved up every penny in order to pay his own way. When he was twenty-one he entered the École des Beaux-Arts and the studio of Gleyre, where he made friends with Monet, Sisley, and Bazille.   He accompanied them on their outings; together they went to Chailly in the forest of Fontainebleau, where, in 1864, he met Diaz.   Despite the intervention of Corot and Daubigny, his work was rejected at the Salon of 1866.   He fell under the influence of Courbet and Fantin; the portrait of *Lise* (1868) is the first work which affirms his own personality.   Life was difficult, but his good humor sustained him.   With Sisley, Bazille, and Monet he worked along the banks of the Seine at Bougival, where he painted *La Grenouillère* (1869),   When war was declared he was conscripted, sent first to Bordeaux and then to Tarbes; but immediately upon the cessation of hostilities he returned to Paris, went back to work with Sisley in Bougival and Louveciennes, and often visited Monet at Argenteuil.   Durand-Ruel, to whom he was introduced in 1873, bought his first pictures, which enabled him to set up in a large studio in Montmartre, at 35 Rue Saint-Georges.

RENOIR. WOMAN SEATED ON THE GRASS. 1895. GANGNAT COLLECTION, PARIS.

As the Salon stubbornly remained closed to him, he joined his friends in the first of the group's exhibitions at Nadar's (1874). At the public auction in the Hotel Drouôt, which he had organized with Monet, Sisley, and Berthe Morisot, ten of his canvases failed to bring in even a hundred francs. The help of the collector Chocquet and of the publisher Charpentier kept him going. A trip to Italy in 1881 acquainted him with the works of the Italian primitives and of Raphael, and he slowly began to break away

245

from Impressionism. He admired Ingres and for some time adopted an extremely meticulous method of painting in which drawing played the dominant role. Nevertheless, after 1890, he returned to a less dry and more expansive style. As if obsessed by the female body, his principal subjects were usually nudes. He continued to make frequent trips both in France and abroad, but the precarious state of his health and the rheumatism with which he was afflicted forced him, after 1899, to retire to Cagnes in the Midi. In 1904, the retrospective exhibition of his work at the *Salon d'Automne* was an affirmation of his triumph. He continued to paint despite an attack of paralysis in 1912 which deprived him of the use of his limbs and obliged him to work in an armchair with his brush attached to his hand. He died at Cagnes on December 3, 1919. Renoir had renounced Impressionism—he had even spoken to Vollard of his "hatred of Impressionism"—because he considered himself primarily as the successor of those whom he had first admired—Boucher and Fragonard—the painters of the eighteenth century. "Because Fragonard laughed, everyone quickly said that he was a minor painter; for me a picture must say something pleasant, joyful, and pretty, yes pretty. There are enough tiresome things in life without our having to make more."

ROUART, Henri. Born in Paris, 1833; died there, 1912. The son of an old Parisian family, Rouart occupied a position of more importance among the Impressionists than his work would lead one to suppose. His wealth and urbanity, his cultured taste, both as a man and as a collector, allowed him, where his painter friends were concerned, to fill an unobtrusive but necessary role—that of a man who could help them and could alleviate their material difficulties without ever appearing obtrusive. He had known Degas at the lycée; he renewed their friendship in 1870 and became like a brother to him. When the aging artist became almost blind and increasingly misanthropic, he found a warm welcome in Rouart's house in the Rue de Lisbonne. Paul Valéry, who in his youth was a frequent visitor to the house, wrote: "He [Rouart] loved only those true values which he could appreciate in more than one field. The same man who was one of the leading collectors of his time, who appreciated and, very early, acquired works by Millet, Corot, Daumier, Manet—and El Greco—owed his fortune to his mechanical constructions, to his inventions which he carried from the realms of pure theory to that of technique, and from technique to industrial practicability. . . ." From the beginning, Henri Rouart shared in all the vicissitudes of the Impressionist group and, since he exhibited with them seven times, was one of their most faithful associates. But because he allowed himself to become thoroughly absorbed by business he was unable to devote the necessary time to painting, and today he is considered a minor painter.

S E U R A T , Georges. Born in Paris, 1859; died there, 1891. Seurat did not live to see the consequences of his idealistic concentration on research and his patient labors. Son of a court attendant, he first attended a municipal art school, then, for two years, the École des Beaux-Arts (1878-1880). Seeking to discover the secret of Veronese, Ingres, and Delacroix, he believed that he would find it in Chevreul's study of "the simultaneous contrast of colors." Between 1881 and 1883, he devoted himself primarily to drawings. His first large canvas, *Une Baignade,* was rejected by the jury of the 1884 Salon, and so he helped to precipitate the formation and was one of the founding members of the *Société des Artistes Indépendants,* presided over by Odilon Redon. He allied himself with Signac and, together, they created the technique of Neo-Impressionism. For them it was a question of rejecting Monet's empiricism and of constructing something ratio-

nal and scientific, of finding an infallible recipe of every master-piece. With the systematic approach which is typical of him, Seurat worked very slowly; it took him two years to paint *Un Dimanche d'Été â la Grande Jatte* (1884-1886) which required at least thirty studies in oil and twenty-seven preparatory drawings. His principal works were *La Parade* (1887-1888), *Les Poseuses* (1887-1888), *Le Chahut* (1889-1890); his sudden death on March 29, 1891, at the age of thirty-two, prevented him from completing his final work, *Le Cirque*. "At the time of Seurat's death," said Signac, "the critics acknowledged his talent, but maintained that he had left not a single work. It seems to me, on the contrary, that he gave, and gave superbly, all that he had to give. He would certainly have produced much more and would have developed, but his task was accomplished. He had surveyed everything and had established, almost definitively, the use of black and white, harmony of line, composition, and the contrast and harmony of color. What more can one ask of a painter ?"

SIGNAC, Paul. Born in Paris, 1863; died there, 1935. The son of well-to-do parents, Signac began to paint at an early age. At fifteen, he copied the works of Manet and made sketches after Degas. A fervent admirer of Monet, he went to him for advice, and Signac's first landscapes reveal Monet's influence. When he was twenty-one he took part in founding the *Société des Artistes Indé-pendants* (1884) where he came to know Seurat, who was exhibiting *Une Baignade*. Captivated by the divisionist technique, he decided to collaborate with Seurat and to formulate the principles of the style baptized "Neo-Impressionism" by Fénéon. Camille Pissarro (briefly), Charles Angrand, Lucie Cousturier, H.-E. Cross, Maximilien Luce, Hippolyte Petitjean, and Théo van Rysellberghe all joined this new group. As John Rewald says, it was Signac who was the driving force of the group, particularly after Seurat's death in 1891. Enthusiastic, impetuous, and hearty, Signac felt it imperative to spare no pains, to convince, to be of help. He visited every port from Holland to Corsica, went to Italy and Constantinople, settled at Saint-Tropez, and at each of these places he painted water colors which are vibrant with spontaneity. From these he created, with meticulous care, large and scientific canvases, trying always to obtain "the most harmonious, luminous, and colorful result. " In *From Delacroix to Neo-Impressionism* (1899) he set down his profession of faith, the Neo-Impressionist charter; he also wrote a study of Jongkind and numerous articles. From 1908 on he presided over the *Société des Indépendants* for twenty-six years.

S i s l e y , Alfred. Born in Paris, 1839; died in Moret-sur-Loing, 1899. Born of British parents, Sisley spent all his life in France, apart from a few infrequent visits to London. After a half-hearted venture into commerce he joined Gleyre's studio (1862), where he made friends with Monet, Renoir and Bazille, and with them discovered the delights of the French landscape. His essentially poetic feeling for nature, both dream-like and delicate, evoked memories of Daubigny, Lépine, and Corot. In London, in 1871, he met Durand-Ruel who sponsored an important exhibition of his works in 1883. Financially ruined by the death of his father, he still went on painting. Marly, Bougival, Louveciennes (1872-1876), Sèvres, Suresnes, Saint-Mammès (1877-1882), and Moret, where he finally settled, are the motifs which he repeated tirelessly with the same feeling of melancholy. From 1885, more and more influenced by Monet, he adopted the Impressionist technique and colors. Leading an extremely with drawn existence, he became touchy and irritable and allowed himself to remain practically unknown among his generation. "He watched all the joys of life depart from him one by one, except the joy of painting, which remained always." He died of cancer of the throat on January 19, 1899.

T o u l o u s e - L a u t r e c , Henri. Born in Albi, 1864; died in Malromé, 1901. Born into the old French aristocracy he was brought up in the Château de Malromé by a pious mother and a father devoted to falconry, horses, and hunting. He was educated in Paris at the Lycée Condorcet, but his already delicate health was further undermined by two successive falls which left him an invalid. Even when he was a small child he used to draw and, on the advice of Princeteau, a friend of his father and a painter of animals, he devoted himself to painting. In 1882, he went to Bonnat's studio in the École des Beaux-Arts where his master found his drawing "atrocious"; then he went to the studio of Cormon. At that time he painted like Bastien-Lepage and Lewis Brown, but he also made the acquaintance of Émile Bernard, Anquetin, and Van Gogh, who impressed him greatly. His friends helped him discover bohemian Paris, the Paris where social outcasts were able to live a free life. In 1884, he set himself up in the Rue Tourlaque in Montmartre, not far from the studio of Degas. Thenceforth, the "Mirliton" and the " Moulin Rouge" were like home to him. Valentin le Désossé, Jane Avril, Grille d'Égout, La Goulue, Casque d'Or—young women who today are known only by their nicknames—became his friends. He illustrated Bruant's songs, drew posters, and decorated La Goulue's booth at the Foire du Trône (1895). The sentimentality of the underworld left him untouched. An aristocrat through and through, he was drawn to people who were out of the ordinary regardless of their origins, and he applied himself to defining them without any of the cruelty of Degas, yet at the same time without moralizing. He painted them "as they were," devoid of mis-interpretation and double entendre. Passionately interested in horses, both because of his background and because they were incarnations of the very essence of beauty—nobility, elegance, power, and speed—he could be found in the paddock at Long-champ by day and in the bar of the "Moulin Rouge" at night. But the alcohol which ate into his system and his disordered life left him prey to the most terrifying obsessions. He was sent to a mental hospital in Neuilly (1899) to take a cure for alcoholism. It was during his stay in the clinic that he executed—from memory—the famous series of drawings of the circus. Struck down by an attack of paralysis at the age of thirty-seven, he died in his mother's arms in the Château du Malromé on September 9, 1901.

VAN GOGH, Vincent. Born in Groot-Zundert (Holland),

1853; died in Auvers-sur-Oise, 1890. Van Gogh was descended from a long line of pastors; two of his uncles were art dealers. At the age of sixteen, he went to work for one of his uncles who managed a branch of Goupil's art gallery in The Hague. Four years later he joined the London branch of the same firm, but after some differences with the manager of that firm he was sent to the main office in Paris. Disgusted with the art business, he told his employers that their profession was nothing else than "organized theft," and showed only pictures he himself liked to prospective customers. He was discharged after seven months. In 1876 he returned to England, where he became an assistant teacher in Ramsgate, a job which lasted only nine weeks. After his return to Holland, he worked in a bookstore for three months, and when this, too, failed to work out, his father permitted him to go to Amsterdam and matriculate at the theological faculty of the university. After a year's study he had to admit failure. He attended a missionary school for three months prior to going to the Borinage mining area to spread the word of God. After six months, during which he led a life of fanatical asceticism, the church authorities recalled him. Poor and miserable, he became "nostalgic for painting" and enrolled in the Brussels academy of arts. Deeply shaken by an unhappy love affair, he painted somber pictures full of despair. Having failed to pass the entrance examination of the Brussels academy, he went to The Hague to work with his cousin, the painter Mauve. After two years of extreme poverty, he returned to the parsonage of his parents.

After the death of his father, Vincent moved to Antwerp where he attended the local academy. In February, 1886 he left for Paris, where his brother Theo was living. There, at the studio of Cormon he met Anquetin, Toulouse-Lautrec and Émile Bernard. His brother introduced him to Pissarro, Degas, Gauguin, and other members of the Impressionist group, and under their influ-

VAN GOGH. SELF-PORTRAIT OF THE ARTIST WITH A PIPE. 1889.
MR. AND MRS. LEIGH B. BLOCK COLLECTION, CHICAGO.

ence Vincent began to use the light colors of Impressionism; for a time he even experimented with the Pointillist technique of Neo-Impressionism. In Amsterdam he had already come across Japanese prints, and in Paris he copied works of Hiroshigé and Kesai Yeisen.

Van Gogh, becoming conscious of the pitfalls and weaknesses of the Impressionist technique, did not remain in the Impressionist camp for long. The petty disputes of the Parisian artists, the negative public reaction to his paintings which found no customers, and, finally, a fight with his brother Theo (who helped him so generously)—all these events combined to make Paris unpalatable for him and he decided to move to the south of France.   His brother Theo agreed to continue to support him.

On February 21, 1888, Vincent arrived in Arles.   The sun-drenched landscape enchanted him.   He remained in Arles for fifteen months and during that period he painted more than two hundred pictures.   Yet it was not a period of unmixed joy.   The allowance given him by Theo, who had married and faced some financial problems himself, hardly paid for paints and brushes, and for weeks at a time Vincent would suffer pangs of hunger.   Also, the local population was extremely hostile, dubbing him the "mad

VAN GOGH. THE TOWN HALL AT AUVERS. 1890.
V. W. VAN GOGH COLLECTION, LAREN.

painter." On October 20, Gauguin, summoned by Vincent, arrived at Arles. The two friends worked together, but they had numerous squabbles, and on Christmas Eve, after a fight in a local inn, they broke off forever. After that, Van Gogh frequently would lie in wait for Gauguin, razor in hand. Ultimately, he used the razor on himself, cutting off his ear. Gauguin left Arles and Van Gogh was hospitalized for two weeks. After his release he suffered a renewed attack of insanity, and at the urging of the citizenry of Arles he was once more hospitalized. After this second attack, Van Gogh voluntarily committed himself to the asylum of Saint-Rémy. Theo agreed to bear the costs of this confinement.

At Saint-Rémy, Vincent continued to work prodigiously, but the pictures painted there bear the unmistakable traces of insanity: restless, tortured lines, unsteady compositions, burning colors. After spending a year at Saint-Rémy he moved to Auvers-sur-Oise to the house of Dr. Paul Gachet, an enthusiastic art lover and collector. Initially, everything seemed to go well there, and he created an enormous number of dramatic, colorful canvases. But after a while he fell out with Dr. Gachet and also with his selfless brother.

On July 17, 1891—on a Sunday—Vincent shot himself. Two days later he died in the arms of his brother Theo.

WHISTLER, James A. McNeill. Born in Lowell, Mass., 1834; died in London, 1903. His father, of Irish origin, was an army engineer. Attracted by the army as a career, the young Whistler went to West Point in 1851. But his love of independence clashed with school discipline and he soon left the Academy. Subsequently, he became a map engraver with the U.S. Coast and Geodetic Survey, but in 1855, incapable of conforming to anything that did not appeal to him, he gave that up also and left America for Europe to devote himself to painting. Bohemian Paris welcomed and overwhelmed him. He enrolled with Gleyre and made friends with Degas, Legros, Bracquemond, and Fantin. Courbet and Manet helped and advised him. Like the other Impressionists, he tried to gain acceptance by the Salon, but he suffered successive setbacks in 1859, 1860, and 1863. He exhibited his *The White Girl* in the *Salon des Refusés* in 1863. From 1859 on he lived mainly in London—mostly in Chelsea—and achieved considerable success in England as a portrait painter and etcher. The influence of Velasquez is apparent in many of his portraits, but Whistler gave them a delicacy, an exquisiteness of color and composition, derived in part from Japanese art. Like the Impressionists, he reacted against anecdotal subject matter in painting. He held that nature contains the elements, in color and form, of all pictures as the keyboard contains the notes of all music; that the artist is born to pick and choose and group these elements scientifically and that the result may be beautiful. This conception of painting is exemplified above all in the series of *Nocturnes* which he began in the 1870's—mostly views of the Thames at night based on observation but painted from memory, with shadowy silhouettes of the banks or the bridges and delicate patterns and color harmonies. These did not meet with the approval of Ruskin, whose harsh criticism brought on a libel suit by Whistler. Whistler won his case but was only awarded one farthing damages. He was declared bankrupt and left for Venice in 1879, returning to London the following year. Honors began to come to him in the 1880's: in 1886 he was elected President of the Society of British Artists; in 1889 he received a first-class medal at the Paris International Exhibition and was made Chevalier of the Legion of Honor; in 1891 the portrait of his mother was purchased for the Luxembourg Museum in Paris. Dandified and belligerent, he adopted the butterfly as his emblem and wittily castigated his enemies— above all the critics—in his "The Gentle Art of Making Enemies."

CHRONOLOGY

	POLITICAL AND SOCIAL SCENE	LITERATURE AND MUSIC
1855	Paris World Exhibition. Crimean war: Fall of Sevastopol to the Allies.	Alexandre Dumas fils: *Le Demi-Monde.* Walt Whitman: *Leaves of Grass.* Ivan Turgenev: *Rudin.* Matthew Arnold: *Poems: Second Series.* Charles Kingsley: *Westward Ho !* Death of Charlotte Brontë.
1856	Treaty of Paris. War of Britain and France against China. War between Britain and Persia.	Victor Hugo: *Les Contemplations.* Ralph Waldo Emerson: *English Traits.* Herman Melville: *Piazza Tales.* Richard Wagner: *Die Walküre.*
1857	British and French take Canton. Indian Mutiny (Sepoy Rebellion). Peace of Paris between Britain and Persia.	Charles Baudelaire: *Flowers of Evil.* Gustave Flaubert: *Madame Bovary.* William Makepeace Thackeray: *The Virginian* Anthony Trollope: *Barchester Towers.*
1858	Attempted assassination of Napoleon III (Orsini Plot). Indian Mutiny suppressed. Treaty of Tientsin. Compact of Plombières (Napoleon III, Cavour). Beginning of War of the Reform in Mexico.	Ivan Goncharov: *Oblomov.* Jacques Offenbach: *Orpheus in the Underworld*
1859	Franco-Austrian war. Battle of Solferino, Austrian defeat. Armistice of Villafranca. Ferdinand de Lesseps begins construction of Suez Canal. John Stuart Mill: *On Liberty.* Death of Metternich.	Charles Dickens: *A Tale of Two Cities.* George Eliot: *Adam Bede.* Wagner: *Tristan and Isolde.* Charles Gounod: *Faust.*
1860	Anglo-French expedition in China. Treaty of Peking. Tuscany, Modena, and Parma join Sicily. Lincoln elected President of the U.S.A. Nightingale Training School for Nurses founded in London.	Eliot: *The Mill on the Floss.* John Ruskin: *Modern Painters* (last volume).

PAINTING	TECHNOLOGY AND SCIENCE	
...ejected by the World Exhibition, Courbet shows his pictures in his *Pavillon du Réalisme*. These cause a scandal, but make a great impression on Pissarro, Manet, and Degas.	Robert Bunsen: Bunsen burner. Henry Bessemer: Process for converting iron into steel. David Edward Hughes: Type-printing telegraph.	**1855**
...anet leaves Couture's studio. ...egas visits Italy. ...ssarro works in Montmorency. ...illais: *The Blind Girl*. ...ourbet: *Two Girls on the Banks of the Seine*.	Wilhelm Zenker: Color photography.	**1856**
...illet: *The Gleaners*. ...onet, then 17 years old, draws caricatures at Le Havre. ...anchester Art Treasures Exhibition.	Louis Pasteur: Experiments with fermentation.	**1857**
...onet meets Boudin at Le Havre. ...enoir paints on porcelain. ...eath of Hiroshigé.	First Transatlantic cable completed.	**1858**
...ssarro and Monet at the Académie Suisse. ...anet's paintings rejected by the Salon.	Charles Darwin: *On the Origin of Species*. James Clark Maxwell: Theory of electromagnetic field. Rudolf Virchow: Cell theory.	**1859**
...ourbet opens a studio. ...egas: *Young Spartans Exercising*. ...onet in Algeria on military service. ...ézanne studying law at Aix; Bazille medicine at Montpellier.	Asphalting of roads. Construction of London Underground begun. Étienne Lenoir: Internal-combustion engine.	**1860**

POLITICAL AND SOCIAL SCENE	LITERATURE AND MUSIC
1861 Outbreak of American Civil War. Italian unification: Cavour. Victor Emmanuel II King of Italy. Confederate States of America formed; Jefferson Davis its president. Emancipation of serfs in Russia. French intervention in Mexico. Death of Prince Albert, Cavour.	Eliot: *Silas Marner*. Dickens: *Great Expectations*. Hans Christian Andersen: *Fairy Tales*. *Tannhäuser* produced in Paris.
1862 Bismarck becomes Prussian premier. Foundation stone of new Paris Opera laid. Lincoln issues Emancipation Proclamation.	Hugo: *Les Misérables*. Leconte de Lisle: *Poèmes Barbares*. Turgenev: *Fathers and Sons*. Death of Thoreau.
1863 Polish insurrection suppressed by Russia and Prussia. Mill: *Utilitarianism*. Denmark annexes Schleswig.	Ernest Renan: *Life of Jesus*. Henry Wadsworth Longfellow: *Tales of Wayside Inn*. Henry David Thoreau: *Excursions*. Death of Thackeray.
1864 Geneva Convention (Red Cross). First International founded by Karl Marx. Austro-Russian War against Denmark; Denmark cedes Schleswig-Holstein. Octavia Hill begins housing-reform program. Lincoln re-elected. Maximilian crowned emperor of Mexico.	Cardinal Newman: *Apologia pro Vita Sua*. Anton Bruckner: *First Symphony*. Robert Browning: *Dramatis Personae*. Feodor Dostoevski: *Notes from the Underground* Death of Nathaniel Hawthorne.
1865 Assassination of Lincoln. Fourteenth Amendment to the Constitution of the U.S.A. abolishes slavery. William Booth founds the Salvation Army.	Leo Tolstoi: *War and Peace*. Lewis Carroll: *Alice in Wonderland*.
1866 Seven Weeks' War; Austria defeated by Prussia at Battle of Sadowa. Italy annexes Venetia. North German Confederation formed.	Émile Zola: *Mon Salon* (dedicated to Cézanne) Doestoevski: *Crime and Punishment*. Henrik Ibsen: *Brand*. Bedrick Smetana: *The Bartered Bride*. Johannes Brahms: *A German Requiem*.

PAINTING	TECHNOLOGY AND SCIENCE	
anet represented at the Salon by *Spanish Guitar Player ;* he becomes fried of Baudelaire. ssarro, Cézanne, and Guillaumin at the Académie Suisse. erthe Morisot becomes a pupil of Corot.	Gustav Kirchhoff and Robert Bunsen: *Spectrum Analysis.* Ernest Solvay: Process for making soda from common salt.	**1861**
anet: *Music at the Tuileries ;* he meets Degas. onet spends the summer at Le Havre with Boudin and Jongkind. the Gleyre Studio: Monet, Renoir, Sisley, Bazille. illiam Powell Frith: *The Railway Station.*	Alfred Nobel uses nitroglycerine as an explosive.	**1862**
lon des Refusés: Scandal created by *Le Déjeuner sur l'Herbe.* onet, Renoir, Sisley, and Bazille leave the Gleyre Studio and work at Fontainebleau. histler: *The White Girl* shown at *Salon des Refusés.*	Sir Charles Lyell: *The Antiquity of Man.* William Bullock: Rotary press. Thomas Henry Huxley : *Evidence as to Man's Place in Nature.*	**1863**
ntin-Latour: *Hommage à Delacroix.* egas: Several portraits of Manet. zanne, his pictures rejected by the Salon, returns to Aix. onet at Honfleur with Boudin, Jongkind, and Bazille.	William George Armstrong: Recoil cylinder. Werner von Siemens: Dial telegraph.	**1864**
anet: *Olympia ;* he travels in Spain, discovers Velasquez. sarro exhibits at the Salon. onet: *Le Dejeuner sur l'Herbe ;* works with Renoir and Sisley at Marlotte.	Gregor Mendel: Experiments on plant hybridization. Joseph Lister works on antisepsis.	**1865**
anet: *The Fifer* refused by the Salon. gas: Racing scenes at the Salon. sarro at Pontoise. onet: *Camille* at the Salon; works at Ville-d'Avray. ntings by Cézanne and Renoir refused by the Salon. zille: First version of *Family Reunion.*	Ireland-Newfoundland Transatlantic cable.	**1866**

POLITICAL AND SOCIAL SCENE	LITERATURE AND MUSIC
1867 Austro-Hungarian Dual Monarchy formed (*Ausgleich*). Emperor Maximilian executed in Mexico. Alaska Purchase. Paris World Exhibition. Second Parliamentary Reform Bill in Britain. Marx: *Das Kapital*, I. British North American Act: Canada becomes Dominion. Disraeli British Prime Minister.	Gounod: *Romeo and Juliet*. Ibsen: *Peer Gynt*. Zola: *Thérèse Raquin*. Death of Baudelaire.
1868 Revolution in Spain. France adopts parliamentary system; freedom of press and assembly granted.	Wagner: *Die Meistersinger von Nürnberg*.
1869 Suez Canal opened. College for women founded at Cambridge. German Social Democratic Party founded.	Arnold: *Culture and Anarchy*. Wagner: *Das Rheingold*. Dostoevski: *The Idiot*. Francis Parkman: *The Discovery of the West*. Mark Twain: *Innocents Abroad*. Death of Charles Augustin Sainte-Be Alfonse de Lamartine.
1870 Dogma of Papal infallibility. Franco-Prussian War. September 4: Third Republic proclaimed in Paris. Siege of Paris.	Eugène Fromentin: *Les Maîtres d'autrefois* Jules Verne: *Twenty Thousand Leagues under Sea*. Death of Dickens, Dumas père, Jules De C court.
1871 Treaty of Frankfurt. March 18-May 28: Paris Commune. Thiers elected President of France. William I crowned emperor of Germany. Rome becomes capital of Italy.	Zola begins *Les Rougon-Macquart*. Arthur Rimbaud: *Le Bateau Ivre*. Eliot: *Middlemarch*. Giuseppe Verdi: *Aïda*.

PAINTING	TECHNOLOGY AND SCIENCE	
net: *The Execution of Maximilian;* exhibits all his rejected works in a gallery in the Place de l'Alma. sarro, Monet, Renoir, Sisley, Bazille, and Cézanne rejected by the Salon. net: *Women in the Garden.* llet: *The Angelus.* ath of Ingres.	Siemens: Dynamo. Christopher Latham Sholes: Typewriter. First lift, at Paris Exhibition.	**1867**
rot: *Woman with Pearl.* net meets Berthe Morisot; he exhibits *Portraits of Zola* at the Salon; paints *The Balcony.* noir: *Eliza;* portraits of *Sisley* and *Bazille.* net works at Étretat, exhibits at Le Havre. zille: Second version of *The Family Reunion.*		**1868**
net and his friends frequent the Café Guerbois; he paints *Lunch in the Studio.* sarro at Louveciennes. net and Renoir work at Bougival. hibition at Munich: Courbet *(The Marsh)*, Manet, Leibl.	Dimitri Mendelejeff demonstrates existence of "periodic law" in relationship between elements.	**1869**
tin-Latour: *Studio at Les Batignolles.* net, Degas, Renoir, and Bazille in the army; death of Bazille at Beaune-la-Rolande. zanne at L'Estaque. Pissarro and Monet in England.	Siemens: Electric furnace. Jean Martin Charcot: Hypnosis used in the study of psychopathology.	**1870**
urbet, president of the *Commission artistique* of the Commune, forced to seek refuge in Switzerland. sarro and Monet, in London, meet Durand-Ruel.	Darwin: *The Descent of Man.*	**1871**

	POLITICAL AND SOCIAL SCENE	LITERATURE AND MUSIC
1872	Spanish Civil War. France pays heavy war indemnities. Germany expells Jesuit order; beginning of *Kulturkampf*. Death of Giuseppe Mazzini.	Samuel Butler: *Erewhon*. Dostoevski: *The Possessed*. Death of Théophile Gautier.
1873	Economic crises in Europe, America, and Australia. Thiers resigns; MacMahon becomes President of French Republic. Proclamation of republic in Spain. Three Emperors' League formed. Death of Napoleon III, Mill.	Arnold: *Literature and Dogma*. Verne: *Around the World in Eighty Days*. Death of Edward Bulwer-Lytton.
1874	Legislation in Britain and France governing conditions of work in factories. Switzerland adopts universal male suffrage. Spanish monarchy re-established. Occupation of Formosa by Japan.	Paul Verlaine: *Romances sans Paroles*. Johann Strauss: *Die Fledermaus*. Modest Moussorgsky: *Boris Godunov*. Wagner: *Die Götterdämmerung*. Verdi: *Requiem*. Flaubert: *The Temptation of St. Anthony*.
1875	Republican Constitution established in France. Universal Postage Union. England acquires Suez Canal shares.	Tolstoi: *Anna Karenina* (1875-1878). Bizet: *Carmen*. Death of Bizet, Kingsley.
1876	First International dissolved. Primary education made compulsory in England. Serbia and Turkey at war. England and France assume joint financial control of Egypt.	Mark Twain: *The Adeventures of Tom Sawyer* Duranty: *La Nouvelle Peinture*. Stéphane Mallarmé: *L'Après-midi d'un Faun* Eliot: *Daniel Deronda*. Death of George Sand.
1877	Queen Victoria crowned Empress of India. Russo-Turkish War: Treaty of San Stefano. Death of Thiers.	Zola: *L'Assommoir*. Ibsen: *The Pillars of Society*. Brahms: *Second Symphony*.

PAINTING	TECHNOLOGY AND SCIENCE	
ıtin-Latour: *A Corner of the Table.* .net in Holland, admires Frans Hals. gas works at the Paris Opera, painting musicians ınd dancers. ·sarro, Cézanne, and Guillaumin at Pontoise. ınet at Argenteuil until 1878. ınoir and Sisley visit him frequently.	George Westinghouse: Automatic air-brake. Death of Morse.	**1872**
.net: *Le Bon Bock ;* meets Mallarmé. gas in New Orleans. ·sarro works at Pontoise, also goes to Auvers-sur-Oise, to Dr. Gachet, where Cézanne is living; *(The House of the Hanged Man).* ley at Marly, Louveciennes and ·ugival. Morisot at Mauricourt.	Maxwell: *A Treatise on Electricity and Magnetism.* Death of Justus von Liebig.	**1873**
·st exhibition of the Impressionist group at Nadar's; ·only Manet not represented. Monet exhibits *Impression, Sunrise.* ınet, Renoir, and Monet at Argenteuil; they become acquainted with Caillebotte.	Heinrich Schliemann: *Trojan Antiquities.*	**1874**
·zanne meets Chocquet. ·sley: *The Flood at Port-Marly.* ınet in Venice ·eath of Corot, Millet.	Death of Lyell.	**1875**
·cond Impressionist exhibition; neither Manet nor Cézanne participate. ınet: Portrait of Mallarmé. ·onet: The *Gare de St. Lazare* series (1876-1877). ·enoir: *The Swing ; Le Moulin de la Galette.* ·zanne at L'Estaque. ·eath of Fromentin.	Alexander Graham Bell: Telephone. Robert Koch: Discovery of anthrax-causing micro-organism. Nikolaus Otto: Four-stroke cycle.	**1876**
·hird Impressionist exhibition; only Manet not represented. ·ssarro and Cézanne at Pontoise and Auvers. ·auguin meets Pissarro. ·sley at St. Mammès-sur-Loing. ·histler begins his *Nocturnes* series; his work is attacked by Ruskin, then Slade Professor at Oxford. ·eath of Courbet.	Thomas Alva Edison: Phonograph.	**1877**

	POLITICAL AND SOCIAL SCENE	LITERATURE AND MUSIC
1878	Paris World Exhibition. Congress of Berlin. Sovereignty for Serbia and Rumania; partial independence for Bulgaria.	Duret: *Les Peintres Impressionnistes.* Thomas Hardy: *The Return of the Native.* Gottfried Keller: *Züricher Novellen.* Henry James: *Daisy Miller.*
1879	Jules Grévy French President; French economic recovery. Zulu War. Dual Alliance (Germany, Austria).	Ibsen: *A Doll's House.* Dostoevski: *The Brothers Karamazov.* George Meredith: *The Egoist.* August Strindberg: *The Red Room.* Peter Ilich Tchaikovsky: *Eugen Onegin.*
1880	Britain at war with Transvaal. French Socialist Party founded. Death of Benjamin Disraeli.	Zola: *Nana.* Tchaikovsky: *Pique Dame.* Henry Adams: *Democracy.* Death of Flaubert, George Eliot.
1881	Czar Alexander II assassinated. Tunisia becomes French Protectorate. American Federation of Labor founded.	Guy de Maupassant: *The House of Mme. Tellie* Verlaine: *Sagesse.* Ibsen: *Ghosts.* Henry James: *The Portrait of a Lady.* Jacques Offenbach: *Tales of Hoffmann.* Death of Thomas Carlyle, Dostoevski.
1882	Triple Alliance (Germany, Italy, Austria). Primary education in France compulsory and secular. Death of Garibaldi and Gambetta.	Wagner: *Parsifal.* Death of Emerson, Longfellow, Trollope.

PAINTING	TECHNOLOGY AND SCIENCE	
onet at Vétheuil, Sisley at Sèvres, Cézanne at L'Estaque. urat enters the École des Beaux-Arts. n Gogh preaches among the miners of the Borinage.	David Edward Hughes: Microphone. Pasteur: *Les Microbes*.	**1878**
urth Impressionist exhibition; fifteen artists, including Degas, Pissarro, Monet, and Gauguin (who exhibited a sculpture), participate. anet: *George Moore at the Café de la Nouvelle Athènes*. gas meets Mary Cassatt. noir: *Mme. Charpentier and her Children* accepted by the Salon. ath of Daumier.	Edison: Incandescent lamp. Ernst von Siemens: First electric railway. Death of James Clerk Maxwell.	**1879**
fth Impressionist exhibition; eighteen artists, including Degas, Pissarro, Morisot, and Gauguin participate. ssarro, Degas, and Cassatt work together, doing engravings. an Gogh begins to paint.	Darwin: *The Power of Movement in Plants*.	**1880**
xth Impressionist exhibition; thirteen artists, including Degas, Pissarro, Morisot, and Gauguin participate. ciété des Artistes Français formed. anet seriously ill. ssarro at Pontoise with Cézanne and Gauguin. enoir goes to Italy, impressed by Raphael and by Pompeii. He then goes to Algeria.	First central electric light power plant opened in New York.	**1881**
etrospective exhibition of Courbet's paintings at the École des Beaux-Arts. eventh Impressionist exhibition; eight participants, including Pissarro, Monet, Renoir, Sisley, Morisot, Gauguin. anet: *The Bar of the Folies-Bergère ;* he is elected Chevalier of the Legion of Honor. ézanne at L'Estaque with Renoir, then alone at Jas de Bouffan. isley at Moret-sur-Loing. urand-Ruel in financial difficulties. eath of Gabriel Dante Rossetti.	Robert Koch: Tuberculosis bacillus. Death of Darwin.	**1882**

	POLITICAL AND SOCIAL SCENE	LITERATURE AND MUSIC
1883	Mahdi Rebellion in Sudan. Annan and Tonkin become French Protectorates. Kruger President of South African Republic. Fabian Society founded. Factory Act in England. Franco-Chinese War. Death of Marx.	Joris Karl Huysmans: *L'Art Moderne*. Friedrich Nietzsche: *Thus Spake Zaráthustra*. Robert Louis Stevenson: *Treasure Island*. Death of Turgenev, Wagner.
1884	French Trade Unions recognized by legislation. St. Gotthard Tunnel opened. Universal male suffrage in Britain. Somaliland becomes British Protectorate. South West Africa becomes German Protectorate.	Huysmans: *À Rebours*. Ibsen: *The Wild Duck*. Brahms: *Fourth Symphony*. Alphonse Daudet: *Sappho*. Mark Twain: *The Adventures of Huckleberry F* Death of Charles Reade, Smetana.
1885	Gold discovered in Transvaal. Gordon killed at Khartoum. German acquisition of East Africa.	Arnold: *Discourses in America*. Zola: *Germinal*. Jules Laforgue: *Complaintes*. Walter Pater: *Marius the Epicurean*. Dujardin founds the *Revue Wagnérienne*. Meredith: *Diana of the Crossways*. Harry Becque: *La Parisienne*. Guy de Maupassant: *Bel-Ami*. Death of Victor Hugo.
1886	Bonaparte and Orléans families banished from France. Statue of Liberty given by France to U.S.A. British acquisition of Burma and the Gold Coast.	Fénéon: *Les Impressionnistes en 1886*. Jean Moréas: *Manifeste du Symbolisme*. Rimbaud: *Les Illuminations*. Zola: *L'Œuvre*. Henry James: *The Bostonians*. Hardy: *The Mayor of Casterbridge*. Ibsen: *Rosmersholm*. Death of Emily Dickinson, Franz Liszt.

PAINTING	TECHNOLOGY AND SCIENCE	
...et at Giverny. ...oir: *Dancing at Bougival.* ...guin gives up his job at the bank and follows ...issarro to Rouen. ...at: *Bathing at Asnières.* ...and-Ruel exhibits Impressionists at Boston, Rotter-...am, and Berlin. ...ibition of Japanese prints at Petit's. ...th of Manet.	First skyscraper (ten stories high) built in Chicago. Klebs-Löffler bacillus (diphtheria).	**1883**
...ospective Manet exhibition at the École des Beaux-...rts. ...of Manet's studio. ...*té des Vingt* founded at Brussels. ...arro living at Évagny, near Gisors. ...et stays at Bordighera, Menton, Étretat. ...guin goes to Denmark. ...on, Signac, and Seurat found the Salon des Indé-...endants. ...vard Burne-Jones: *King Cophetua and the Beggar Maid.*	Ottmar Mergenthaler: Linotype. Charles Parsons: Steam turbine. Koch: Cholera bacillus. Hiram Stevens Maxim: Machine-gun. Death of Mendel.	**1884**
...arro, influenced by Seurat and Signac, adopts Divi-...onism. ...nne at Gardanne during the autumn and winter. ...oir: Studies for the *Bathers.* ...at works on *La Grande Jatte.* ...Gogh at Nuenen: *The Potato Eaters.*	Pasteur: Hydrophobia vaccine. Karl Benz: First automobile powered by internal-combustion engine.	**1885**
Impressionist exhibition : seventeen exhibitors, ...cluding Pissarro, Degas, Morisot, Guillaumin, ...auguin, Signac, and Seurat. ...Gogh arrives in Paris in February. ...nne quarrels with Zola about *L'Œuvre.* ...guin meets Émile Bernard at Pont-Aven, becomes ...iendly with Van Gogh in Paris. ...et, Pissarro, Degas, Renoir, Sisley, Morisot, and ...eurat exhibited in New York by Durand-Ruel. ...at: *La Grande Jatte.* ...ndation of the New English Art Club; acceptance ...f Impressionist influence in England. ...th of Monticelli.	Henrich Hertz: Electric-amgnetic waves. Reginald H. Fitz identified, named, and analyzed appendicitis.	**1886**

POLITICAL AND SOCIAL SCENE	LITERATURE AND MUSIC
1887 Golden Jubilee of Queen Victoria. President Grévy resigns as a result of financial scandals; Boulanger's *coup d'état* fails; Carnot becomes French President. China cedes Macao to Portugal. First Colonial Conference in London. British annex Transvaal.	Mallarmé: *Poésies.* Edmond and Jules de Goncourt: *Journal des court.* Strindberg: *The Father.* Beginning of Théâtre Libre in Paris. Verdi: *Otello.* Anton Chekhov: *Ivanov.* Death of Laforgue.
1888 William II Emperor of Germany. County Councils established in Britain. First railway in China.	Strindberg: *Miss Julie.* Richard Strauss: *Don Juan.* Nicolai Rimsky-Korsakov: *Scheherezade.* Ibsen: *The Lady from the Sea.* Death of Matthew Arnold.
1889 Paris World Exhibition. Suez Canal made neutral and international. Second International founded in Paris. British South Africa Company formed.	Paul Bourget: *Le Disciple.* Maurice Barrès: *Un Homme Libre.* Henri Bergson: *Essai sur les Données Imméa de la Conscience.* Bjornstjerne Björnson: *In God's Way.* Richard Strauss: *Death and Transfiguration.* Gerhart Hauptmann: *Before Dawn.* Death of Robert Browning.
1890 Anglo-French agreement on Nigeria. First International Congress for the protection of workers in Berlin. Free elementary education in England. Resignation of Bismarck.	Ibsen: *Hedda Gabler.* Knut Hamsun: *Hunger.* Pietro Mascagni : *Cavalleria Rusticana.* Stefan George: *Hymnen.* Death of César Franck, Cardinal New Offenbach.

PAINTING	TECHNOLOGY AND SCIENCE	
iguin in Martinique from April until November. i Gogh *(View from Vincent's Room)* and Toulouse- Lautrec adopt Pointillism. trec paints his *Portrait of Van Gogh.* iac "discovers" Collioure.	John Dewey: *Psychology.* Death of Kirchhoff.	**1887**
iet at Antibes. i Gogh at Arles: *The Anglois Bridge, Boats on the Beach,* *unflowers.* ind visit of Gauguin to Pont-Aven with Bernard id Laval; he rejoins Van Gogh in Arles in October, iuarrels violently with him. Gogh enters hospital. rat: *La Parade, Les Poseurs.* nard, Vuillard, M. Denis, and Sérusier at the icadémie Julian. ert joins the New English Art Club. in: *Burghers of Calais.*	John Boyd Dunlop: Pneumatic bicycle. W. S. Burroughs: Adding machine. Pasteur Institute founded in Paris. Emile Berliner: Disc record.	**1888**
oir: *Les Baigneuses.* iet organizes a petition to secure the admission of *iympia* to the Louvre. iguin and the Symbolists at the Café Volpini. iac visits Van Gogh in March. Gogh enters the St. Remy asylum in May; paints *iarry Night.* trec: *Moulin de la Galette.* Nabis group founded. ibition by French Impressionists in London. roup from the New English Art Club exhibits under ie title "The London Impressionists."	Eiffel Tower constructed. Herman Hollerith: Punch-card machines. Francis Galton: *Natural Inheritance.*	**1889**
iet: *Haystacks* series. arro parts with the Neo-Impressionists. inne begins the *Card Players* series. Gogh at Auvers; commits suicide in July. iat at Gravelines; exhibits *Le Chahut.* ich in Paris, meets Gauguin and Toulouse-Lautrec. in: *La Danaïde.*	Emil von Behring: Sero-therapy. William James: *Principles of Psychology.* Koch: Tuberculin.	**1890**

POLITICAL AND SOCIAL SCENE	LITERATURE AND MUSIC
1891 Franco-Russian Alliance: French squadron at Kronstadt. Papal Encyclical on Labor. Antisemitic pogroms in Russia. Nyasaland becomes British Protectorate.	Oscar Wilde: *The Picture of Dorian Gray.* William Morris: *News from Nowhere.* Arthur Conan Doyle: *The Adventures of Sherlock Holmes.* Gustav Mahler: *First Symphony.* Frank Wedekind: *The Awakening of Spring.* Hardy: *Tess of the D'Urbervilles.* Death of Goncharov, Melville, Rimbaud.
1892 Dual Alliance (France and Russia). Leo XIII orders French Catholics to accept the Republic.	Ruggiero Leoncavallo: *Pagliacci.* Maurice Maeterlinck: *Pelléas et Mélisande.* Ibsen: *The Master Builder.* Gerhart Hauptmann: *The Weavers.* Rudyard Kipling: *Barrack-Room Ballads.* George Bernard Shaw: *Widowers' Houses.* Claude Debussy: *L'Après-midi d'un Faune.* Death of Renan, Tennyson, Whitman.
1893 Franco-Russian commercial treaty and military convention. Panama Trial in Paris. Keir Hardie forms British Independent Labour Party. Chicago World's Fair. Death of MacMahon.	José-Maria de Heredia: *Les Trophées.* Adolf von Hildebrand: *The Problem of Form.* Wilde: *Salomé.* Verdi: *Falstaff.* Tchaikovsky: *Symphonie Pathétique.* Giacomo Puccini: *Manon Lescaut.* Death of Gounod, Tchaikovsky, De Maupassant.
1894 Sino-Japanese War. Carnot, French President, assassinated; succeeded by Casimir-Périer. Dreyfus Case. Coronation of Nicholas II of Russia.	Anatole France: *The Red Lily.* Richard Strauss: *Till Eulenspiegel.* Shaw: *Candida.* Bruckner: *Ninth Symphony.* Death of Robert Louis Stevenson, Pater.
1895 Treaty of Shimonoeki ends Sino-Japanese war. Confédération Générale du Travail (federation of trade unions) formed. London School of Economics founded.	Verlaine: *Confessions.* Émile Verhaeren: *Les Villes Tentaculaires.* Theodor Fontane: *Effi Briest.* William Butler Yeats: *Poems.* Wilde: *The Importance of Being Earnest.* Richard Strauss: *Thus Spake Zarathustra.* Death of Dumas fils.

PAINTING	TECHNOLOGY AND SCIENCE	
Monet: *Poplars* series. Gauguin goes to Tahiti. Retrospective Van Gogh exhibition at the *Salon des Indépendants*. First Toulouse-Lautrec poster (for the Moulin Rouge). Death of Seurat, Jongkind.	Edison: Kinetoscope. British Institute of Preventive Medicine founded. Edward Goodrich Acheson: Carborundum. Otto Lilienthal: Glider.	**1891**
Exhibition of Renoir, Pissarro, and Degas at Durand-Ruel. Retrospective Seurat exhibition at *Salon des Indépendants*. Cézanne at Fontainebleau. Signac at St. Tropez. Exhibition by the Nabis at the Barc de Boutteville. Whistler and Burne-Jones exhibitions in London.	Rudolf Diesel: Internal-combustion engine. Death of Werner von Siemens.	**1892**
Monet begins his *Rouen Cathedral* series. Gauguin returns to Paris from Tahiti and exhibits at Durand-Ruel. Matisse and Rouault at the Guastave Moreau Studio.		**1893**
Caillebotte bequest to the Louvre temporarily lodged at the Musée du Luxembourg. Cézanne with Monet at Giverny, meets Clemenceau. Gustav Geffroy publishes his *Histoire de l'Impressionnisme*. The Yellow Book: reproductions of Steer, Sickert, Conder, Max Beerbohm, and Aubrey Beardsley.	Death of Von Helmholtz, Hertz.	**1894**
Cézanne exhibition at Vollard's, Rue Laffitte (150 canvasses); this exhibition influenced the Nabis. Renoir in London and Holland. Gauguin returns to Tahiti. Death of Berthe Morisot.	Louis and Auguste Lumière: Cinematograph. Wilhelm Röntgen: X rays. Death of Huxley and Pasteur.	**1895**

	POLITICAL AND SOCIAL SCENE	LITERATURE AND MUSIC
1896	France annexes Madagascar. Emperor William sends congratulatory telegram to President Kruger (implying German recognition of Transvaal independence). Holland adopts universal male suffrage. Vilfredo Pareto: *Cours d'Économie Politique*. Italian-Abyssinian War.	Marcel Proust: *Pleasures and Regrets*. Chekhov: *The Sea-Gull*. Bergson: *Matter and Memory*. Valéry: *An Evening with Mr. Teste*. Puccini: *La Bohème*. Hardy: *Jude the Obscure*. Death of Verlaine, Bruckner.
1897	Turco-Greek War. Queen Victoria's Diamond Jubilee. Second Colonial Conference in London.	Mallarmé: *Divagations*. Gide: *Les Nourritures Terrestres*. Edmond Rostand: *Cyrano de Bergerac*. H. G. Wells: *The Invisible Man*. Death of Brahms, Daudet.
1898	France occupies Fashoda. Start of Spanish-American War. Zola: *J'accuse* (the Dreyfus Affair). Norway adopts universal male suffrage. U.S.A. annexes Hawaii.	Wilde: *The Ballad of Reading Gaol*. Richard Strauss: *Ein Heldenleben*. Death of Mallarmé, Burne-Jones, Fontane, Moreau, Lewis Carroll.
1899	Start of Boer War. *Action Française* founded. End of Spanish-American War. British Federation of Trade Unions formed. Hague Peace Conference. Second Dreyfus trial.	Chekhov: *Uncle Vanya*. Shaw: *Caesar and Cleopatra*. Death of Becque.
1900	Paris World Exhibition. Boxer Rebellion in China. British Labour Party founded.	Tolstoi: *Resurrection*. Gabriele D'Annunzio: *The Flame of Life*. Joseph Conrad: *Lord Jim*. Shaw: *Three Plays for Puritans*. Puccini: *La Tosca*. Theodore Dreiser: *Sister Carrie*. Death of Ruskin, Wilde, Nietzsche.

PAINTING	TECHNOLOGY AND SCIENCE	
ssarro in Rouen. auguin writes *Noa-Noa*. autrec exhibition at the Manzi-Joyant Gallery. ugo von Tschudi and Max Liebermann buy pictures from Durand-Ruel for the Berlin National Gallery. andinsky and Jawlensky in Munich. eath of Millais, Leighton, William Morris.	Marconi: First patent for wireless tele-graph. Antoine Becquerel: Discovery of radio-activity in uranium. Death of Lilienthal and Nobel.	**1896**
ssarro in London. egas at Montauban. npressionist exhibitions in London and Stockholm. pening of the Tate Gallery in London.	First diesel engine built. William Ramsay: Isolation of helium. Joseph Thomson: Discovery of element-ary particles smaller than atoms.	**1897**
ssarro: *Views of Rouen*. enoir at Essoyes. egas gives up oil painting for pastel and sculpture. auguin: *What are we? Where have we come from? Where are we going?* e Douanier Rousseau: *The Sleeping Gipsy*. odin: *Statue of Balzac. The Kiss.* eath of Boudin, Beardsley, Burne-Jones, Puvis de Chavannes.	Pierre and Marie Curie: Radium. Marconi: First wireless communication between France and England. James Dewar: Liquefication of hydrogen. Death of Bessemer.	**1898**
ignac: *From Delacroix to Neo-Impressionism*. enoir returns to Cagnes. ssarro: *Views of Paris*. oulouse-Lautrec's series of circus drawings. atisse and Derain at the Carrière Studio. abis exhibition at Durand-Ruel. erain and Vlaminck at Chatou. eath of Sisley.	Beginning of atomic physics. Death of Mergenthaler, Bunsen.	**1899**
etrospective Seurat exhibition at the *Revue Blanche*. aurice Denis: *Hommage à Cézanne*. icasso goes to Paris, is influenced by Steinlen and Toulouse-Lautrec.	Max Planck: Quantum theory. Ernest Rutherford and Frederick Soddy study radioactivity. First Zeppelin built. Sigmund Freud: *The Interpretation of Dreams*. Death of Lenoir.	**1900**

	POLITICAL AND SOCIAL SCENE	LITERATURE AND MUSIC
1901	President McKinley assassinated; succeeded by Theodore Roosevelt. Commonwealth of Australia formed. Death of Queen Victoria.	Kipling: *Kim.* Thomas Mann: *Buddenbrooks.* Strindberg: *The Dance of Death.* Death of Verdi.
1902	End of Boer War. Combes Ministry continues anticlerical policy in France. Anglo-Japanese Alliance.	Rainer Maria Rilke: *Buch der Bilder.* Verhaeren: *Les Forces Tumultueuses.* Gide: *The Immoralist.* Hilaire Belloc: *Path to Rome.* Debussy: *Pelléas et Mélisande.* Maxim Gorky: *The Lower Depths.* Death of Zola, Butler.
1903	Investiture of Pope Pius X. Bolshevist-Menshevik split of Russian socialists. U.S.A. acquires Panama Canal Zone.	Romain Rolland: *Life of Beethoven.* Shaw: *Man and Superman.* Henry James: *The Ambassadors.* Arnold Schönberg: *Gurrelieder.* Death of Hugo Wolf.
1904	*Entente Cordiale* (Great Britain and France). Japan declares war on Russia.	Rolland: *Jean-Christophe.* Puccini: *Madame Butterfly.* Chekhov: *The Cherry Orchard.* Death of Dvorak, Chekhov.
1905	Separation of Church and State in France. End of Russo-Japanese war. Revolution in Russia. Norway dissolves union with Sweden.	Wilde: *De Profundis.* Richard Strauss: *Salomé.* Shaw: *Major Barbara.* Death of Verne.
1906	Clemenceau's first Ministry. First Duma (Russian parliament) dissolved. British Labour Party formed.	Rilke: *The Love and Death of Cornet Christop Rilke.* John Galsworthy: *A Man of Property.* Death of Ibsen.

PAINTING	TECHNOLOGY AND SCIENCE	
rospective Van Gogh exhibition in Paris. ond visit to Paris of Picasso; start of his "blue eriod." ath of Toulouse-Lautrec.	First Nobel Prizes. First Transatlantic wireless. Joseph Everett Dutton: Discovery of organism causing sleeping sickness.	**1901**
rospective Lautrec exhibition at the *Salon des Indé- endants* and at Durand-Ruel. uguin writes *Avant et Après, Racontars d'un Lapin*. anne: *Girl with Doll*. net: *Waterloo Bridge*.	Rolffs: Rotary gravure press. William James: *The Varieties of Religious Experience*. *Oliver Heaviside:* Theory of conducting layer in upper atmosphere. Valdemar Poulsen: High-frequency arc. Death of Virchow.	**1902**
n d'*Automne* founded. pressionist and Neo-Impressionist exhibition at the Viennese Secession. no Cassirer publishes *Kunst und Künstler*, a forum or Impressionism in Berlin. ath of Pissarro, Gauguin, Whistler.	Orville and Wilbur Wright: make first powered flight.	**1903**
net exhibits his series *Views of London*. tisse at St. Tropez with Cross and Signac. asso installs himself in Paris at the Bateau-Lavoir. ath of Fantin-Latour, Watts.	Rubel: Offset printing (litho). John A. Fleming: Diode rectifier tube.	**1904**
trospective Manet exhibition at the *Salon d'Automne*. on des Indépendants* exhibits Seurat, Van Gogh. th of Fauvism *(Salon d'Automne)*. tisse: *Luxury, Peace, and Voluptuousness*. Brücke founded at Dresden; beginning of German Expressionism.	Albert Einstein: Special theory of relativity. First dreadnought.	**1905**
uguin exhibition at the *Salon d'Automne*. asso begins *Les Demoiselles d'Avignon*. ath of Cézanne.	Frederick Gowland Hopkins: First studies of vitamins.	**1906**

LIST OF ILLUSTRATIONS

A color plate is indicated by an asterisk (*).

279

THE ANGLOIS BRIDGE. 1888.
Reed pen. 9½ × 12⅝ (24 × 32).
G. Gard de Sylva Collection, Los Angeles. P. 151
WHITEWASHED COTTAGES AT
SAINTES-MARIES. 1888.
Reed pen. 11¾ × 18½ (30 × 47).
V. W. van Gogh Collection, Laren. P. 155
*SELF-PORTRAIT OF THE ARTIST WITH
A PIPE. 1889.
Oil. 20½ × 17¾ (51 × 45).
Mr. and Mrs. Leigh B. Block Collection, Chicago
P. 253

SUNSET NEAR SAINT-RÉMY. 1889-1890.
Pencil. 18½ × 24⅜ (47 × 62).
Neue Staatsgalerie, Munich. P. 167

WHISTLER, JAMES.

*OLD BATTERSEA BRIDGE: NOÇTURNE
—BLUE AND GOLD. c. 1865.
Oil. 26 × 29⅝ (66 × 50).
Tate Gallery, London. P. 48

SELECTED BIBLIOGRAPHY

CANADAY, John: *Mainstreams of Modern Art,* New York: H. Holt & Co., 1959; London: Thames & Hudson, 1959.

ELGAR, Frank: *Van Gogh. A Study of His Life and Work,* Translated by James Cleugh, New York: Frederick A. Praeger, 1958; London: Thames & Hudson, 1958.

GARDNER, Helen: *Art Through the Ages,* New York: Harcourt, Brace & Company, 1959; London: G. Bell & Sons, 1959.

HAMILTON, George Heard: *Manet and His Critics,* New Haven: Yale University Press, 1954; London: Oxford University Press, 1954.

HENDY, Philip: *The National Gallery,* New York: H. N. Abrams, 1955; London: Thames & Hudson, 1955.

HUNTER, Sam: *Modern French Painting, 1855-1856,* New York: Dell Publishing Co., 1956.

LAVER, James: *French Painting and the Nineteenth Century,* New York: Charles Scribner's Sons, 1937; London: B. T. Batsford, 1937.

LEYMARIE, Jean: *Impressionism,* Translated by James Emmons, 2 vols,, Skira, 1959.

MEIER-GRAEFE, Julius: *Entwicklungsgeschichte der Modernen Kunst,* 3 vols., Munich: R. Piper, 1914.

PISSARRO, Camille: *Letters to His Son Lucien,* New York: Pantheon Books, 1943; London: Kegan Paul & Co., 1944.

READ, Herbert: *A Concise History of Modern Painting,* New York: Frederick A. Praeger, 1959; London: Thames & Hudson, 1959.

REWALD, John: *The History of Impressionism* (bibl.), New York: The Museum of Modern Art, 1946.

— *Post-Impressionism from Van Gogh to Gauguin* (bibl.), The Museum of Modern Art, 1956.

ROTHENSTEIN, John: *The Tate Gallery,* New York: H. N. Abrams, 1958; London: Thames & Hudson, 1958.

— *The Moderns and Their World,* London: Phoenix House, 1957; New York: Philosophical Library, 1958.

SCHMIDT, Paul Ferdinand: *Geschichte der Modernen Malerei,* Stuttgart: W. Kolhammer, 1952.

SLOANE, Joseph C.: *French Painting Between the Past and the Present,* Princeton: Princeton University Press, 1951; London: Oxford University Press, 1951.

VAN GOGH, Vincent: *Complete Letters,* 3 vols., Greenwich: New York Graphic Society, 1959; London: Thames & Hudson, 1959.

INDEX